JOB CODES

Iwu Nnadozie Kingsley

DEDICATION

This book is dedicated to the memory of my late father, Mr. Iwu Chinaka Vincent who was killed on duty and to my mother, Mrs. Iwu Emerewa Eunice who sacrificed so much to help us the children, find purpose in life.

ABOUT THE BOOK

This book "Job Codes" aims to balance the emotional well-being of workers and help them recognize their value in the industry. It creates awareness of potential negative challenges and emotional pains that may arise from job tasks, while reinforcing the strength needed to achieve a balanced emotional life. This book is especially useful for individuals striving to become great by starting with small jobs for survival.

ABOUT THE AUTHOR

Iwu Nnadozie Kingsley hails from Umuhu, Ngor-Okpala Local Government Area of Imo State and obtained his BSc in Economics from Chukwuemeka Odumegwu Ojukwu University.

PREFACE

This book was designed to educate, encourage, strengthen, and help workers stay focused, irrespective of the challenges, problems, and pain associated with their jobs, especially those who start with low-paying jobs to survive in the economy, particularly in African countries.

This book addresses common challenges, effects, and pains related to jobs, emphasizing resilience. It aims to serve the interests of workers and guide them on how to be successful in their careers.

The book is divided into fourteen chapters, each discussing factors that create problems for workers and how to build the strength to overcome challenges faced by workers in African countries today. It focuses on four major issues affecting workers and more.

This write-up is based on observations and experiences related to the problems and strengths in the Nigerian job industry, labor market, and labor rewards, especially for workers in Menial jobs. It is not intended to discourage workers in the industry or promote laziness but to help them understand their employment purposes, values, and the risks they take to achieve good results. It encourages workers to recognize their potential and ability to deliver excellent results and understand the challenges they might face while doing their jobs. It also aims to inspire employers to adopt a win-win approac

ACKNOWLEDGEMENT

My special thanks to Almighty God for His infinite mercy, guidance, and protection throughout the period of writing this text.

My profound gratitude to Dr. Korode Oluwatosin, consultant in gynecology and pediatrics and the chairman of Standard Life Care Hospital, Mr. Oliver Ebeh, former account officer of Society Family Health, and Mrs. Lovelyn Solomon Martins, general manager of Kel Technologist Limited, for their fair play and encouragement in the labor industry, fostering a win-win mindset.

To my lecturer, Mr. Clement Sunday Ifebuolili Ezeanyeji (Prof), for your outstanding skills and dedication to lecturing students, promoting the possibility of good industries through study and research.

To Mrs. Ibukunoluwa G. Omodara, for proofreading and contributing valuable insights to this book.

And finally, to the many individuals who contributed to making this book a reality.

JOB CODES:

JOB JOURNEY

JOB ATTITUDE

JOB CHALLENGES

JOB PAIN

AND

IT'S RESILIENCE

WITH

MENIAL JOBS

IN AFRICA

Table of Contents

DEDICATION 2

ABOUT THE BOOK 3

ABOUT THE AUTHOR 4

PREFACE 5

ACKNOWLEDGEMENT 6

CHAPTER ONE 10

JOB AND BOSS 10

CHAPTER TWO 34

JOBS AND CO-WORKERS 34

CHAPTER THREE 50

JOB, FASHION AND SOCIAL LIFE STYLE 50

CHAPTER FOUR 56

THE EFFECTS AND PAIN BEHIND JOB SUCCESS 56

CHAPTER FIVE 60

JOBS, AGE AND GENDER CONTRADITIONS IN NIGERIA CULTURES AND BELIEFS 60

CHAPTER SIX 64

JOB MISSION AND VISION 64

CHAPTER SEVEN 68

JOB AND RELIGION 68

CHAPTER EIGHT	72
RANKS AND SETTINGS IN THE ORGANIZATION	72
CHAPTER NINE	76
JOB AND PAY	76
CHAPTER TEN	86
JOB AND STRENGTH	86
CHAPTER ELEVEN	100
JOB AND SELF-SECURITY	100
CHAPTER TWELVE	102
JOB AND HEALTH	102
CHAPTER THIRTEEN	106
WORKER'S PERSONAL PROBLEM	106
CHAPTER FOURTEEN	112
TRIBALISM AND NEPOTISM	112

CHAPTER ONE

JOB AND BOSS

One of the biggest problems at work can be coming from your boss by never being pleased with the job results no matter how you put in your best. Whatever workers do and how they go about their job success even with profitable results they still have reasons to complain and feel never satisfied. This can be because they never want you to know your value in the company and industry. The only way they think they can go about it is to belittle your work and make workers feel unprofessional on their jobs. The boss will pretend not to be satisfied with workers' results despite their best in the company. Which is known to be selfish or self-centeredness from the boss.

The job becomes very stressful, discouraging, boring and lack excitement, despite the love and passion for the job, as a result of the boss inability to appreciate, recommend, empower, encourage and recognize workers efforts. This type of problem usually affects workers confidence and potentials despite workers' greatness and transforming results in the company. Peradventure you find a way to another company where you will be appreciated; you definitely discover how wonderful and worthy you are in the labor market.

Some boss will make workers receive their entitlement or bonus as company implemented as a favor coming from them whereas it is the worker's right. They feel making you receives it as a right might cost them to increase the worker's salary and increase disloyalty and ability to control them as they want to.

In some cases, a worker will find a situation where their boss use another co- worker against them, this implies that the boss will be using one of the workers against the other workers in order to carry on their selfish interest by cheating, oppressing and over laboring workers, in this scenario the boss play a sleeping force to aim his result on workers while the favorite worker plays active and direct oppressor to his co-worker claiming that it is the nature of the job.

Some of these bosses will go as far as telling their workers to isolate themselves from people in the name of working with them so as to see an atmosphere of achieving their purpose without care of what isolation might cause in their life. We all know that isolation causes loneliness and can make life feel empty by not having the privilege to know and to discover your values and your worth.

Most of these bosses have learned how to consume workers time without considering their families and social life.

WORKERS WEAKNESS

Most time at work workers often complain that their boss is a difficulty person and it is the most challenging aspect of the job. The facts that we need money to run our day-to-day activities which will motivate and enable us to tolerate and do everything possible in the job despite the difficulties or challenges coming from the boss.

you need to understand that in life most humans are selfish, if some humans are selfish, they always want to have their ways of doing things especially in the work space with our bosses, they over labour and cheat their workers, of which it supposed to be a win and win transaction, some bosses are also selfish in job distribution, he or she will always want to rations workers under his control to get maximal products target that will enable the company to stand out in profit without internalizing or paying for extra time.

There are different ways in which the boss can be the problem rather than the job itself. Understanding your boss's personality can be very helpful in knowing how to behave on the job. Bosses can be very logical, and this trait becomes evident from the beginning of your employment. When a worker gets hired, the boss often seeks to gather in-depth information about the worker's personal life, especially during the early stages. They may ask questions about your state of origin, marital status, living arrangements, and family background. For example, they might inquire, "Where are you from? Are you married? Do you live with your parents? Are your parents alive?" These questions can help the boss form a clearer picture of who you are outside of work, which can influence how they manage and interact with you.

Most times when such questions like this come up, you feel it is an opportunity for you to gain sympathy by answering all the questions; many workers even go far by commenting on their problems, having no idea you are giving more power over you to your boss. This will be the beginning of your boss taking control and advantage of you. You have assisted your boss to move to the second stage questions which is logical; your boss will put the information to use and takes steps ahead of you as a worker. What the boss is trying to capture is your reasoning and ability, after getting all this information the boss now has an edge over you. To make it simple, the boss can now detect your level of reliability in the job or how your life depends on the job for survivor. It will make the boss to add more responsibility without adding to the pay or wages and any little mistakes from you the boss will be threaten to sack you.

I usually advise people to know how to answer these questions, some of these questions seem to be harmless to you but very important to your boss, answer by putting on a little smile and if there is need to answer those questions, answer them in an implicit manner not in details. If your boss persists in knowing tell your boss that it's confidential and personal to you. Those questions that are not related to the job that might belittle you or affects your effort, answer some of these questions by saying "everything is okay" or "they are okay" If it is a must to answer correctly, put it in a way your boss will see confidence in you.

There is a time to share such kind of stories with the boss but at first you must understand the kind of boss you are working with, if you have to discuss such with him/her definitely not on the early stage. This reminds me of my experience when I was working as a driver, my few days at work my boss asked me if I was a graduate, I said "yes". He further asked;

"What discipline?"

I responded, he tried to engage me on my study (discipline) which I was very happy discussing some fact about my course. For some few days at work I felt my boss will be a very good boss and I hoped he might be of help to me in getting a better job. An incident occurred one faithful day, he told me to stop driving and park, aside my inability not to hear him quick I parked a little bit ahead, suddenly he began to shout and said some degrading words. I began to question myself "what is he trying to express and what does me as a graduate has to do with this incident"

that became the beginning of me regretting my actions, assuming I knew, I would have said "No" After the incident occurred, he started to capitalize on me being a graduate as a way of hitting on me. That is how the problem started and I tried doing more to save my job and kept saying

"sorry sir", " sorry sir'

The information given out in a mere discussion has become a weapon in the hands of my boss.

I found out he was not expecting his driver to be a graduate. He was expecting a driver that will work for him for a lesser pay and for a long period of time, if possible a life time. He felt I might get a better job and higher pay because of my qualification which will make me quit and cost him time looking for another driver.

I was angry and replied him "what have I done to you sir? Why is me being a graduate a problem?" he responded "didn't I know that there is no vacancy for graduate in this country? Can't I see many graduates rooming about the street for jobs?" That was how I discovered the problem.

The truth today is that every film wants to employ good workers that will work for years or possible for his or her life sperm even if the organization pays him or her little (fraction) or not.

I had an experience as a sales representative with my boss (madam), she discover I was a good sales representative. One day she asked a question,

"what will you like to do apart from working with me"

I quickly answered "Business" I gave her reasons not knowing she is trying to extract some information. After giving her my answer she no longer feel comfortable with me, she started suspecting me of running my own business while working for her, thinking one day I will leave her business for my own. The moment i answered those questions it became the beginning of my problem.

Avoid telling your boss your family problems, your career plan and be very mindful how you give an answer to your boss questions but if necessary, I encourage workers to always study their boss at first which is the only way you can have an edge, you should always take time to study and understand the kind of boss you work with, which will help inform how far you can go in personal discussion and non-job relative talks with your boss.

Most of these bosses enjoy having good workers but lack how to maintain these workers. Seizing their freedom in the name of being a boss, they try controlling your time, freedom, and life because everything you do will revolve around your work space. As a worker you will continue to labour in the same company without getting your flowers.

They will schedules work in a way that workers will consume more time on the job without having time for other activities and family.

To survive in the hands of your boss in this economy and industry the workers have to be very prudent and wise enough to observe and study the kind of boss they are working with and to know the level and boundaries in between and how to deliver their duties.

UNEMPLOYMENT THREAT IN THE WORKPLACE

The rates of unemployment in Nigerian industry have become a threat to workers, whenever a worker goes for his/her right it comes to their detriment and result to them losing their job. The boss has seen this means as a way of intimidating and weakling the workers instead of seeing such as a way of renegotiating and re-valuing workers services. They see employment as rendering a favour, help or charity. Workers have gradually been devalue to their boss as a result of unemployment high rate, They do not work with time frame as constitution of employment policy state or as the job demand in the employment letter, we work to please the boss with every means and go through a lengthy policy in order to retain their job and pay. Workers should be very careful on how they try to comfort themselves with managing a job or else it will take you out of passion and society.

VALUE FOR YOUR SERVICES NOT ON PROMISES

The capitalist doesn't help so easily workers think; whenever you are working under a capitalist or venture owner have it in mind that what you are doing is trading your services for pay or rendering labor in exchange of reward (wages and salary) not to derive free money from your boss or company owners', do not work with the mentality of expecting your boss to make you rich, rather work good enough to render your services at your best to make your boss pay you enough to make you rich. Bosses have mastered the strategy of making unfulfilling promises especially when you hope on their undocumented promises and under pay.

UNDER PAID JOBS

Under paid jobs are the jobs that pay low or little to labor service rendered and under estimate workers service in labor industry and market. It's advisable you shouldn't settle on low paying job keep moving and advancing in knowledge and skills to aim more, probably from one job to another till you obtain your career job or better paying job. laziness and fear of starting over and moving over to another job have made some workers anticipating on spending all their working age with one firm expecting their boss to reward them greatly during their retiring time. It ends with heart break despite little pay during service without appropriates agreement and good benefits.

The capitalist keeps promising their worker of greater rewards in order to get their best services and most of the great promises will never be fulfill, getting to the period and age workers can no longer deliver best service they used to render, the boss will come up with something else ending it with the company is very sorry but they have to let you go that you can no longer deliver optimum service that deserve your post, they will make you leave without making you great, which many retirees have come to regret their life time spent with a company which have no value for them.

DEVALUE THE VALUABLES

Devalues the valuables are viewed in two ways, first is those values and benefits attached to workers' office, post and position and second are those values and benefits tag to workers' productive value targets.

First among the two are those values and respects that are attached to worker's position and post such as official car with driver, change of wardrobe, vocational tourism and beneficial items. These things are been used by the boss to make workers feel too relax and comfortable with the job even when the job is not really transforming the workers' wants and needs. These packages has made workers to lose concentration with their job career and purpose rather than focusing and concentrating on the benefits of the current job, with colleagues they feel too big, too respected and too superior to come down to a certain level and reasoning with the lowest staff, those things are actually creating issues with workers who lacks understanding or having wrong knowledge on how to handle this situation. When the workers finally lose their job, they get to understand they are far below what the boss made them to be and the type of lifestyle the boss exposes them into has created a difficult hypothesis for the workers to cope with after the job.

For workers to get more value of services remitted to a company and to meet their needs and wants there should be purpose to devalue some of these valuables in order to gain more and to be focused with technics. Too much high concentrations on job position, post, values and gain can deform workers' ability on focusing. For workers to achieve personal value and job career values they need to devalue the unnecessary values that is attached to official post by focusing more on self-purpose, needs and wants of their job career.

Secondly, In this case the boss attaches some values and benefits based on productivity, where workers has to meet up to a certain percentage of results to be able to access these benefits and values. Do you know that your boss is too technical and brave to determine how valuable your job is to you? Your boss will hang the value and benefits where you will be seeing it and it will be difficult to achieve, for possible way of having your loyalty, and get you to work more and eventually work for the company for life, with few workers getting access to such because organizations do not want to lose valuable workers, but by devaluing the valuables it takes the company and boss unaware for workers to achieve their career purpose and job values.

Value and benefits tag to workers' productivity results has create a lot of problems within The work space. It has resulted to hi-jacking of clients from colleagues, penetrating each other's tertiary and lack of trust within co-workers.

Desperate chasing of productivity values and benefits attach to position and post doesn't make workers good fellow despite it increases company's productivity because it stirred unfair game play within workers and the tenacity of workers to become enemies.

Leaving the value and benefits behind while motivated to increase your results and to have good collaboration with your co-workers will aim good productivity and best way to determine your job strength and a peaceful job journey with colleagues. It gives loyalty and respect within workers.

Note: this very important devaluing the valuable shouldn't let you lose value and act according to your post as when due and necessary as demanded even if it demands to be strict at the moment or cautions and to flag reports but not to support the weak workers.

BOSS ORIENTATION

These are earlier training workers under go in the company with the boss and it is conducted by the superior which is the boss itself. It usually based on how the boss will derive his or her selfish interest and to achieve maximize energy, good services, profit and efficiency labor service from the workers with low pay and without win-win game.

The company owners known as boss are so talented and comic especially when it get to what they want; they can go as far as promising what they cannot fulfill, most times in order to get workers fully committed to the job without proper agreement "documentation". During these period of orientation, they often made workers feel free, relax, favored and to feel like family in order to get your interest and energy to gain high productivity for low pay.

At the period of these orientation you feel so blessed, lucky and opportune to make it, by heading to the oral training; the boss will promise if you can do better than they expected, there will be extra percent of money that will be giving to you outside your salary but remember it is not included on the employment letter. They keep promising if you can help in developing the company the company will buy you a car or give you a huge amount of money as compensation annually also you will gain promotion to a higher level that you will never regret working with them, all these oral promises by the boss help to trigger your working ability to work more and be over labored, stressed, and working without sticking to opening and closing time.

Everything about you become work and work even at the level of trading away your social value in order to utilize the opportunity promised by the boss of which you will hardly see a boss who keeps to his promises in Nigeria Africa.

This reminds me of my former boss I once worked with during her orientation training on different occasion, she said she is going to help me if I will be of assistance to develop her business that she is a good person and doesn't have problem, I began to see it as an opportunity to grow or gain promotion I started working with all my energy and resuming before the opening time, closing after the closing time; keeping my families and social activities aside; I began to have my job task possible, my sales was very excellent even the marketing director were commenting about my sales been above target.

One day, very early in the morning I was very sick and I could not go to work my neighbor had to came over to assist me in purchasing some drugs and monitor me to make sure I am better, at my resumption time I wasn't at work, my boss have to call; my neighbor picked the call and told my boss that I'm very sick and may not be able to make it to work, according to him he said my boss replied okay and dropped the call. When it got to 4pm I regained my strength and was imagining how todays sales might be like knowing it might led us to loss on some of sales from my important customers that would not be patient till the next day, I quickly rushed to work since I live close to work to see what I can do. I saw my boss already redistributing to customers I quickly joined her to some extent she said to me even thou I was sick can't I call her rather than keep her business stranded if not that she was around I would have close down her business. I felt pain and I replied her saying;

"Ma, if I had known I would be sick I would have called, you didn't even ask about my health?"

We are talking about life, if not my neighbor who rescued me I would have found it difficult to resume by now she replied me saying ''I don't care how you feel with grievance'' I felt touched with pain in my spirit and imagine the whole sacrifices and effort I have put into her business only to have a sudden brief illness and break down that over powered me, this is all I got to hear I felt unwanted again, to my surprise this is how she gradually refused to fulfill her promises, and all my effort have become wasted.

This experience has taught me no matter how great you are towards your success in the job; your one day failure can change everything. Your boss can be selfish, the day you fail to continue to deliver you become an enemy to the organization. The company can leave you without compensation as they promised and they can forget those days, this is simply to tell you that all boss orientation without documentation can be just to fulfill their selfish interest.

There is a mini supermarket I used to supply and I have good relationship with the manager, one day he was sharing his experience with the company with me; he said the first time he started with the company his boss called him out and told him that if he can develop the company to at least three hundred and fifty thousand naira net profit every month, his salary will be increased and he will make him never regret working in his organization.

Those words has made him to work very hard without scheduling time for himself and family, after the first quarter the supermarket made a net profit value of more than a million naira both in goods with the value of eight hundred thousand naira in store, that he was expecting the boss to be happy and to keep his promises rather the boss was suspecting him to be stealing and not giving accurate value of the profit. His boss started to use his power and position on his table by employing more workers to take part of his job from him and bringing external auditor to audit quarterly. He said he felt heartbroken. The painful part is that the boss refused to fulfill his promises.

He told his boss if you don't want to fulfill your promise at least increase my salary and also he should let him head the new workers, his boss disagreed that if he is tired of the job he can kindly leave that he have stolen enough from him and my friend said he suspected it was his boss friends that was pushing his boss hard on this, My friend was fed-up and discouraged working with the company and he was like I'm tired working with this company, he is gradually looking for somewhere else for a job. After developing his boss business, he sees reasons to make him look regretting of extra and excess commitment.

The causes of this failure from bosses especially one-man business and company for not remitting their promises was as a result of no documentation of the promises in order to force it to be fulfill, if not, they do always see reasons not to fulfill their promise. In every strategy you take that can help you stand out there is this imagination or selfish interest that tells your boss to over throw you and to underestimates you because they always want to have it alone, and it take more knowledge and grace to point out exception among bosses. So as workers make sure your boss internalize his promises into appointment or documentation and signed which will stand as evidence.

SUPERVISORS

These are workers authorized to oversee departments, sectors, or groups within a company to coordinate and meet budget targets. However, some supervisors misuse their power, becoming challenges and problems for their subordinates.

Supervisors have the authority to discipline, correct, and point out weaknesses, but some exploit this power for personal gain rather than the company's goals. They may mistreat and overwork their staff, delegate their own duties to subordinates, and unjustly force workers to remit part of their salaries back to the company through fines and sanctions. Often, these actions occur without the company's knowledge, with supervisors threatening termination to enforce compliance. They may also assign their own tasks to staff to secure personal commendations and provide insufficient time for new employees to adapt to their roles. These supervisors frequently give improper directives, display impatience in training workers, and belittle staff to maintain control, sometimes even exploiting the opposite gender for sexual favors.

Some supervisors overburden and suppress workers, claiming it is the nature of the job. When workers complain about stress and challenges, these supervisors insist it's just how the job is and nothing can be done. However, when a new leader takes over, the previously stressful and difficult job often becomes easier, revealing that the issue lay with the former supervisor's management style, not the job itself.

Workers should not accept demeaning behavior from bullying supervisors. I recall an incident with a senior staff member who belittled my efforts early in my tenure by unfairly comparing my qualifications to another's. I quickly warned her not to undermine my qualifications. Micromanagement by such supervisors makes jobs unnecessarily stressful and hectic.

There are always better ways to manage work to make it conducive for workers, ensuring both the employees and the company succeed. When supervisors manage solely for the company's benefit, it creates undue stress for workers, limiting their freedom and well-being.

LYING AND DENYING WORKERS

We do get shocked and wonder how our boss lie and deny an event despite the scene having an eye witness, the truth is our boss want to be on the good side and success part of the story nothing more nothing less, any other way or things that doesn't contribute to success is unacceptable. The Boss have their way of lying and denying any unproductive moment and result from workers such as they will say I don't know what you are talking about even when they have full knowledge about it, or you are on your own and so on. This lying and denying act by the boss usually comes up whenever workers fail to achieve success on a project signed and authorized to workers under boss directive. Boss lying and denying as if he or she never involved in the failure of the job assigned to worker, even when the boss insisted workers should follows his or her directives.

In some case you expect your boss to consider you based on some ground that you know better but he or she chose to deny you when knowing the cause and reasons why you failed your daily task. They know they contributed to the failure, which blows workers minds by saying the word at least the boss should consider me In front of the co-worker.

The truth about your job and reasons why you are employed is to achieve success in every assignment giving to you because from its success the company will make money and pay your salary that is why when a particular assignment is being assign to a worker, a worker should try his best as possible to make it to success, peradventures you noticed the boss direction is not working for good kindly go back to his office and discuss it over if he or she finds it difficult to accept your initiation carry on and go ahead with his directions and put it to work and at the end, it could be you both arriving at the same results with different ways of remittance but peradventures you see it not going to turn out good make it obvious that you are working under boss directives and order and when it finally turn out unsuccessful make it know to the boss with apology and technics saying it was based on his order, you earlier suggested a way that will be of good result which he declined, if not your boss might be too fast pushing the blames on you and denying you and make you pay for damages or query you. It will create bad record and sometimes the boss does this to get your loyalty for their negative target and if you are a disloyal worker they put fear in you. The boss has to lie about you to weaken your mind, believe and power to get you submissive under his or her instructions for selfish interest purposes.

In other ground if you see the boss directives and orders are not going to contributes to the success You went ahead and put in work until it was obvious that you were working on orders from the boss. When it ends wrong, your boss always has ways to put all the blame on you. All you have to do is find a suitable means of letting the boss know that you followed an order; otherwise, he will keep seeing such scenarios as your inability as a worker. He will keep referring to you as a bad example and never get involved, acting like he did not contribute to the failure through his directives. Failure or an unsuccessful project, in some cases, cost you your job as a worker. You could go beyond the boss's orders to reach the objective of succeeding at your job if you are 100% sure of success, but pretend it was according to the boss's directions. Because some boss does not understand the nature of the job before they become a boss, especially when it comes to a field job, they always want to give unnecessary orders through imagination about what they think rather than what it is in the field. A case that you would also find is where the boss does not give the workers space to concentrate on the job, and the negative energy from the boss is even more than the one coming from the job itself. This might be in the frequency with which the boss distracts calls while passing directives on the job and other ways of interrupting and delaying the job proceedings — barriers or negative impacts that the boss never sees or counts.

AGGRESSIVE TRANSFER ON WORKERS

Some bosses can be very harmful in the way they transfer aggression, using it as a method to indirectly punish workers for perceived offenses or to set up workers they deem disloyal. These bosses often resort to this tactic when they find it difficult to get rid of a stubborn worker under their supervision. They transfer their anger onto certain workers by badmouthing them to the newly appointed boss during the handover of vital documents and information. This malicious behavior can significantly affect the targeted worker's relationship with the new boss, who may act on false information and assumptions.

Overcoming this challenge requires a high level of intelligence because the worker will be penalized for something they are unaware of. The worker may be left wondering what they did wrong to deserve such treatment from the new boss, not realizing that it stems from the previous boss's aggression. This negative mindset can lead the new boss to accept the condemning views of the previous boss, causing further issues for the worker.

The solution lies in the new boss's understanding and the worker's ability to recognize the potential transfer of aggression. If the new boss is capable of seeing through the negativity, they might give the worker a fair chance. It's crucial for the worker to remain professional and strive to build a positive relationship with the new boss, demonstrating their value and dispelling any negative assumptions.

NATURAL HATRED

As humans, we all have a natural aversion that we try to avoid, limit, and control because it makes us unhappy. This dynamic often occurs between bosses and workers. A boss may harbor an inexplicable dislike for a particular worker, making it difficult to manage their interactions and hindering the worker's access to benefits within the boss's control. Only some bosses possess the self-control to rise above these feelings. This situation contributes to the challenges some workers face. It's crucial for workers to be proactive in discussing and renegotiating plans with their bosses to overcome these obstacles. Understanding your boss's attitude towards you helps in anticipating and predicting your position and tenure within the company

THE BOSS ANGER

Anger is natural, though sometimes unwanted or irrational, and emotional that everybody experiences occasionally. Experts in this field describe anger as a primary natural emotion that has evolved as a way of surviving and protecting you from what is considered wrong-doing. While it is advisable for people to learn how to manage anger as humans, since this is a natural source of temper, in order to avoid unacceptable results, some of the bosses will capitalize on anger as a way of intimidating workers into getting loyalty; while on the other hand, some workers have bosses who are quick to anger. In these cases, it becomes too difficult for workers to cope with the boss, and as a result, every worker is afraid of discussing plans with the boss due to his or her quick temper, which will generate embarrassment. On the other hand, the workers also find it difficult and are afraid of seeing their boss every day, which makes the job very challenging for workers who are too emotional to stay in such a job.

We recorded a bad habit that the boss often shouts at workers without reason. Even when they are at their best, the boss still shouts at them, acting as if nothing seems to be good about the workers, making workers feel intimidated, unloved, lacking confidence, fearful, and without a sense of belonging. Workers, for example, who 'belong in' this excrement, keep asking themselves this one question: 'What in the world did the boss want from us? He never gets to sanctified, even at our best. Whenever the boss is walking close by to workers, the workers will lose him or herself due to unwanted manners from the boss.'

This kind of boss believes that doing so will keep the workers fearful, committed, respectful, and able to deliver good work without consideration for the workers' emotional disturbance. The funny thing about this kind of boss is that they know and understand every worker's strength and greatness but still carry on with this bad attitude to make the workers unable to determine the good about themselves and to detect their values in the company and the labor market.

It only requires bold and courageous workers to overcome this kind of boss. As a worker, your mind should never be set on any negative energy coming from a boss that could affect your positive thoughts about the job. Learn how to focus more on good delivery, not on his character, because the boss knows the workers who are performing well. I keep saying this to workers so they can understand and study their boss first before the boss gains the upper hand, to be ahead of the boss and still stay in the position, every boss has their weakness too. Knowing and understanding your boss could make you the only one among workers who can have free flow with them and overpower them. To workers who are emotional in handling this kind of boss, the better option for such workers is to quit that job and find a more peaceful and emotionally stable job.

Just as in my previous place of work, where the boss had the character of being quick to anger and shout at workers, never satisfied with the service of workers; whenever he was around, the security would be fast to inform every worker to comport and behave themselves, and everybody started working in fears and praying for his leave. We lost confidence and shied away whenever the boss walked by or approached any one of us. We did not like him coming to the office. We kept praying that he should have outdoors meetings to attend, and if he traveled, it would seem like a holiday and freedom for all workers; as if there were heavy robes lose around our necks.

DISCIPLINE AND WICKEDNESS

Disciplines are the ways and purposes for correcting workers for their wrong deeds and bringing the job back into shape. The bosses and disciplinary committee see them as an atmosphere to be wicked in trying to maltreat the workers in the name of discipline. How bosses and the disciplinary committee provide the meanings and interpretations of disciplines keep workers wondering and confused regarding what discipline means. Sometime workers are yet to understands the difference between discipline and wickedness, most time the way company narrate and act wickedness and called it discipline baffles the staff but leave them with no option. Yes, it is very good to discipline workers who go wrong in order to shape him or her back in good way but not to devastate them and fuse workers with pain in the name of discipline. The companies create rules and regulations on workers that has no doubt that it is wickedness but they have no option but to carry on with the job keeping their hopes on divine grace of which this has really hurts a lot of workers in this situation; even in some cases you notice some threating words from the boss in the name of discipline which is not encouraging from who supposed to have built the workers on a win and win grounds and goals

SEXUAL ABUSE AND ADVANCEMENT

In Africa today, sexual abuse and advancement have been crazy, and one of the biggest problems and challenges facing the workers in Africa, especially female workers and companies as a whole, from achieving their purpose and goals. Sex has become a tool for job position and delivery, and likewise, for bosses to promote workers, they have to demand sex in exchange for the opposite gender. Many female workers have seen it as a quick and fast way to get to the next stage of the job, promotion, salary increment, and otherwise. This has cost the positive and integrity-filled workers a lot, such as emotional disturbances and killing the job feelings and passion. The problem seems to extend to company growth and development as a result of unmerited promotions and the inability of a boss to control and sanction workers who they are taking sexual advancement advantage of.

In some way, the workers are left with no option but to quit their jobs—undoubtedly one of the most challenging acts to do, especially in a dream job. To fail to accept a one-night stand with the boss or to resign from the job means the boss will get impossible and frustrated, which is the ultimate stress and pain a worker can be put through. Ways of overcoming this have always been complex; it demands that you have a very mature mind and well-organized co-workers to succeed. Remember, the faster you understand your boss the better, for it will help you know how to go about it without losing value. Some workers have given up their hopes in God because of the high pressures coming from the boss. Others see quitting as the solution, and many have had to meet the demands of the boss even if it is not from the heart, especially when the person in question is too mean and curious about their demands—with a lot of threats, intimidation, job pressures, and job unsatisfactions. No other option is left for those workers except quitting, and fear of quitting has made them compromise with the abnormal demand coming from the boss

CHAPTER TWO

JOBS AND CO-WORKERS

Co-workers have ways of provoking, creating problems, and facing challenges with colleagues. No matter how hard they try to make peace with one another, despite their excellent job delivering and portfolio differences, they have ways of injecting negativity into others through their actions and reactions. This may result to hatred, jealousy, intimidation, and unpleasant characters toward one another. These bad takes have cost the lives of many workers and impaired their passion for the job, which is considered a significant issue among co-workers. Generally, such bad attitudes develop emotional pain and jeopardize their mental health conditions, leaving them unhappy most of the time. This is where co-workers become concerned not only with the difficulty of the job task but also with other co-workers challenges, difficulties, and problems arise in the job to ensure that a conducive atmosphere is created for the delivery of satisfactory results.

The worker's good ability and wisdom, in this case, are crucial to handling problems with colleagues and ensuring a good stay at work and an improved way of handling the job for a positive result. The facts and purpose created by their problem might not be viable and realistic. Still, the truth is that it will give you a conscience since it presents an additional phase in the company in question, and it gives a chance that such problems might cost you your happiness or lose your job.

Most of the time, you might respond in grievance, which is probably not the best way to handle such challenges. You know there can be a perfect and logical way through which you can go about it. Maybe, in making your mind achieve this stance by using frustration, you have to be rational and wise in seeking a solution. Know when to listen, when to stop, and look over because your response will not enable management to intervene appropriately, and rightly, which might give rise to warranted judgment that might assume you to be an enemy. The wisdom that you will not rely on a problem from co-workers yet continue to hope and give more reason for solutions will provide you with more credit simply because you wish for a solution. Sometimes a little break with co-workers can lead to a solution; sometimes, it might develop in the tiny space generated by misplacing tools, which will be found in time-space rather than creating differences.

THE INFLUENCERS

Workers should be conscious of the introducers and influencers among co-workers at work. Those are regarded as the smart ones, usually doing illegal deals in the company to add to their income; they will do anything possible to protect that illegal business in the organization. These means of quickly introducing those ways of gaining money are robbing and outsmarting the company. They know well that they cannot accomplish their process without passing through some worker's table. It will become a very challenging time for you as a worker if they find it interesting to pass through your table to accomplish their illegal purposes. They can always find their way by giving you reasons why you need to be part of them to achieve the unlawful business under the shield of the company.

At first, coming to you they always make one feel the company is not enough for you and the company is not going help you to achieve your dream, their conversation are to determine the needs and unsanctified side of workers for them to use such opportunity to introduce their illegal business and get workers part of the illegal business simply because their illegal business is uncompleted without the very worker processes and acknowledgement for faking it look real and part of the company transactions through the worker terms of reference (T.O.R).

Your conversation with them says a lot as a worker during the new days with the company and to determine what next, they will be asking questions like.

"Brother, how do you see your job? Are you married? How far with the salary payment? Hope your transport fare is accommodating?"

Your response determines their next move, they will continue asking questions that will make you feel unsatisfied with your pay and hope to get more, then they go ahead saying even them too and their family are managing the pay and it's not enough, only if there could be any possible way of getting additional money it will be nice, note; your response to questions determine how interested you are, failure to give them a good response makes you an enemy in which they will do everything to set you up and get rid of you in order for them to fulfill their negative and selfish interest only if they have the power.

You should be very careful how you go about making extra money under the company you are working with. These illegal businesses end up taking away workers job most time and one of the most problem workers have is too much interest in making more money rather than the job and salary within.

The funny way of a thief is that they don't think all ways round before going into business they are move by the profit calculation, I do advice people to check and balance before going into illegal business within the company, most time the consequence of such illegal business in will end you paying more than what you steal in value, it can as well go further to keep you stranded in the labor market and industry if care is not properly taken.

All these influences started from your earlier days at work where you notice your co-workers asking you some questions and feeling too conscience especially during leisure time to determine your social ability, questions like "do you drink alcoholic drinks? Do you club?" And you people might be standing outside of the company and you see one of them pointing at a lady passing by and say "see the lady waist?" this is very inviting and the question will be push to you indirectly to hear from you, your inability to tackle this types of question well will give them better way to influence you and to be part of their illegal business, for every illegal business under the company, workers behind such always want to recruit every necessary workers in the company to make a strong hood.

Be very careful how you respond to their question especially your earlier days at work, if possible, lead the game ahead by understanding the kind of workers you work with. The critical aspect of it is that peradventure they introduce such illegal business to you and you say "NO" they will become a threat to you in the organization and set you up to get you out of their way. That is why it is important you have to be ahead of your co-workers which can help you to fight in return and to keep your job in position and to leave them with their selfish interest except the company interest. And take notice any secret you keep with your co-worker can comes to become your weakness in future in the company but if at all you have to keep not the crucial one and always think before you talk at times your colleague come to make you to commit by your words and it will become your weakness and this weakness can take you out of job if not nearly in future. Remember the strength of any worker is the ability to know other workers weakness.

In a critical company there is logical ways of responding to their demand tell them "you are not going to be a problem to their way and your kind of person don't involve in such that please you are very sorry and you promise this conversation is between them". And henceforth you have to be very careful how you carry on your duty for you not to indirectly attend to their deed and never mind how they go about their illegal business.

These remind me of things that occurred in my few days of working with a company as a driver. After entertaining some friendly questions from my co-worker, one day, my boss sent me to go and purchase diesel (gas) in the keg with one of the vehicles. As I was driving out to the gate, one of the security personnel, a "gateman," told me to wait, which I waited for him. He entered the vehicle and said it would be nice to go with me. To me, it would be fun, and I said yes. We both went to the filling station.

On the way, he stopped me and told me to hold on and said, "How much were you given to procure diesel? And how much are we going to buy?" At this point, everything seems clear to me by how smart he is in coming so close and asking me these questions. I told him quickly, "Sorry, I'm not easy like that. It can't happen." Well, he was sorry indeed, very sad, and so emotionally unhappy till we got back to the office. To me, I was thinking "Should I get into this with him? Who knows who he is working for, and who knows what kind of business he will want to introduce me to next?'

The earlier I cut him off, the better. I saw some facial reactions from him, and days later, other co-workers like the gateman colleague, security colleague, and a few office staff was acting differently towards me. That is how I discovered and noticed that it was a routine illegal business done within a few workers in the organization. I usually tell my friends that they should be quick and bold enough to understand their co-workers to avoid falling victim. They also have to talk less and avoid unnecessary organizational prompts, which will help. If in the case one is a type of talkative person, then learning how to speak with intellect and principle will go a long way in helping.

Remember, that not all business is business, that power and authority are exercised only when it is time and needful to do your job. Here, you are good to know that every worker with a tremendous logical term that they are people of different beliefs and purposes while working: they use various ways and forces, such as going as far as taking anybody out of the way if stopped from carrying out or achieving their selfish mindset to make themselves great at work. This is why you must be brave and confident in being logical about how you tackle the situation. Not all businesses are good because workers will want to engage by all means, even on their pay raise due to underpayment in salary.

The kind of business with this should be able to assess the circumstances and whether the organization is interested since, in some companies, one might never know that the waste materials can be converted into money. That reminds me of what happened a few years ago when I was working with one of the nylon industries as a security officer: the company never knew that the waste rubber drum used to bring in liquid raw material could be exchanged for money. Initially, the company was busy throwing it away before security officers noticed people coming around to pick it up for their use.

The demand became so high that most of them were seriously coming to us, the security, and telling us that we should be keeping it for them. That is how we started adding value to the waste drum, and this is how the securities were doing business under the company's shade by selling off the company-wasted drum. We were seriously making reasonable money through it until the time the company found out that we were making money through their waste drum; the management had to call us in order and release a circular that there would be no more throwing away of any drums again. That is how they put a stop to it, and it was added to the company market sales value to generate money for the company.

We also have cases where some workers were stealing from the company's products to sell them eventually and were caught and then arrested. Until my going out of the job as a security officer, I didn't know the way they went about the case, so you have to be warned and get to know not all

Business enterprises are often assumed to be the primary sources of income. However, many people also tend to assume that these sources of revenue are illegal. It is crucial to understand the nature of any business before deciding to engage with it. Take your time to evaluate the costs and benefits of the venture. Engaging in illegal business might bring you money in the short term, but the consequences can be severe. You risk losing everything you have worked for, your career and even your life if you are not careful. Why would you want to get involved in such activities? Remember, you have no excuse for engaging in illegal business in a court of law.

Failure to avoid interacting with individuals who have illegal interests can lead to being set up or tested by such co-workers. For instance, I was once set up by a co-worker. One day, the head of administration asked me to take the company car to a mechanic for servicing, and I was given money for the service and fuel. Unknown to me, my co-worker had conspired with the mechanic to monitor the amount of fuel I would purchase.

After leaving the gate, the mechanic asked for the service money, which I gave to him, this was my first mistake. As we were about to reach the service point, the mechanic reminded me to purchase fuel, which I did in the exact amount. His reminder made me cautious. Upon leaving the filling station, the mechanic revealed that he had been instructed to watch me but suggested we could do business together by selling the car's catalyst and using a cheaper lubricant instead of the recommended one. I refused both suggestions.

After the car was serviced, my co-worker unexpectedly arrived at the workshop. Suspecting foul play, I drove back to the office and reported the incident to the administration. Both the mechanic and I were called in for explanations, and it became clear that I was set up by my co-worker. The administration congratulated me for my sincerity.

You may also encounter workers who group together to plan how to achieve a salary increment and present it collectively to the boss. If the boss dislikes hearing about salary increments, these workers might back down at the last moment, leaving you to face the boss alone. If you lead the discussion, you risk becoming the boss's enemy and being blamed for corrupting other workers' mindsets. This can mark the beginning of your troubles with both the boss and the group of workers who will pretend they had no part in the plan.

In an organization, be strategic about how you approach joint plans with co-workers. Ensure that everyone involved follows through, or be prepared to withdraw quickly. There is nothing wrong with demanding a salary increment if it is based on improved productivity and results. However, if it is a collective plan, make sure it is done logically and collaboratively. Observe carefully, or you might be pushed into a difficult situation.

UNEXPLAINED FORCES IN THE WORKPLACE

Workers come from diverse backgrounds, including different beliefs and religions, and some are pagans. Due to high unemployment rates, many workers struggle to find jobs. This scarcity has led some to resort to using voodoo and spiritual interventions to secure and keep jobs, even when they may be weak or lazy. They use these practices to avoid being fired and to gain promotions within the firm.

One critical aspect to understand about every co-worker is that they come from different religious backgrounds and beliefs. Some use various magical forces to excel at their jobs and might go to great lengths, including harming others, to achieve success. These unexplained forces, often referred to as voodoo, are used by some workers to kill their colleagues, protect themselves, or gain promotion and success in the labor industry, even when they do not deserve such advancements based on their performance. Voodoo can manifest in many ways, including poisoning or spiritually attacking co-workers, inducing illnesses, or using magical powers to gain favor and retain jobs.

Instead of developing their skills and improving their abilities, some workers prefer to rely on these unexplained powers. This behavior has harmed and even killed many workers, causing them to lose their careers. While some people claim they do not believe in such powers due to their faith, the reality is that these powers can have real effects and can backfire on those who misuse them. It is essential to be cautious with co-workers and maintain fair play in all interactions.

Religious faith can play a significant role in countering these unexplained forces. A strong faith, prayer, and commitment to religious principles can provide divine protection, which is believed to be more powerful than any other force. Therefore, workers should focus on their responsibilities and avoid interfering in their co-workers' tasks without consent. This approach fosters good relationships and reduces the likelihood of conflicts that might provoke others to use these harmful powers.

COLLEAGUES INTERVENTION

When I worked as a driver for a private hospital, an incident occurred that highlights the importance of not intervening in co-workers' duties. One day, while washing the managing director's car, I found his expensive cell phone inside. I decided to return it to him after finishing the cleaning. However, as I was about to do so, the secretary arrived and, seeing the phone on the car seat, took it straight to the director's office without informing me.

Such actions can create a misunderstanding and conflicts among workers. If anyone should have reported the cell phone, it should have been me, as it was my responsibility according to my job description. Intervening in other workers' duties can cause quarrels, working relationship, and create animosity. It is best to avoid such actions unless explicitly authorized or when tasks are jointly assigned. Still it has to be with both concepts to collectively achieve the goal.

FRIENDSHIP WITH FEMALE STAFF

This is an important aspect to consider before entering into a relationship or close friendship with a female co-worker, and how to maintain that friendship. Male workers often view female workers as easily approachable or see them merely in terms of their job roles. However, the truth is that female staff may have smaller work responsibilities but are often well-connected to the highest authority, either through kindness or favor. Some bosses feel comfortable discussing family and social issues with female workers, extending beyond job-related matters.

Female staff often receives special attention and privileges from their bosses, which allows them to handle tasks beyond their official job descriptions without being questioned. These relationships are usually confidential, and other staff members might not be aware of the extent of their connections. As a result, a female staff member who appears to be an ordinary employee may actually be highly connected to the boss.

Building a good relationship with female staff can be beneficial. They can advocate for your reputation and promotion because they have direct access to the boss and know how to get the boss to listen to them. However, you need to be careful about how you present your friendship with her. If the boss is having a sexual relationship with her, your closeness might provoke jealousy and lead to dangerous repercussions or animosity from the boss.

This reminds me of an experience during my university days when I had a close female friend. We helped each other with assignments, shared campus information, and had fun together. We even attended extra coaching sessions after lectures. Unknown to me, one of our lecturers had been trying to pursue her romantically, but she kept refusing his advances. The lecturer eventually learned about our close friendship and assumed I was the reason she was rejecting him. He began monitoring our interactions, thinking we were dating, even though we were not. My friend never mentioned the lecturer's advances to me.

During the examination period, we both wrote the lecturer's course, expecting good results. However, when the results came out a month later, I was shocked to see that I had failed. I knew I had done well on the exam and couldn't understand why I had failed. Curious, I contacted some friends to ask about their scores. When I asked my close friend, she also said she had failed. She then revealed to me that the lecturer had been demanding sex from her and blamed me for discouraging her from accepting his advances. I was stunned. She reassured me that she had a plan to address the situation.

In the end, I had to retake the course to pass it. I never found out how my friend resolved things with the lecturer, but I reconsidered my friendship with her after that incident.

At work, a similar situation can arise. If your close female friend is being pursued by your boss and she refuses his advances, the boss might blame you, thinking you are the reason for her rejection. This can negatively impact your relationship with the boss, leading to demotions, unfair treatment, or even job loss, without you knowing the real reason behind it. It's crucial to manage your relationships and friendships with female co-workers carefully to avoid such misunderstandings.

I'm not suggesting that you shouldn't be friends with female co-workers, but be mindful of the potential consequences. Avoid becoming too involved in situations that could lead to misunderstandings and negative repercussions.

Also, it is important not to interfere with female staffs that are having a sexual relationship with the boss. Focus on your assignments and strive to build positive relationships with all co-workers, regardless of gender, to achieve collective goals. Interfering with such relationships can lead to negative outcomes, as illustrated by an incident at a previous job of mine. The company owner was having an affair with the cashier, who was subsequently promoted to an accountant position despite lacking the necessary qualifications. She began exerting control, giving orders, and deciding promotions, transfers, and demotions. Those who opposed her relationship with the boss faced demotions, pay cuts, and even termination. This situation significantly affected the company's dynamics.

JOBS AND ATTRACTION

Love is a beautiful thing, fun and sweet, and it can significantly impact a worker's job. I always tell friends that some of the most common places where people find their spouses are university campuses, places of worship, and workplaces. When you find love or when love finds you at work, it can determine the progress or regress of your job career. Knowing how to manage love at the workplace is crucial. If you are lucky enough to find love at work, it can greatly help in protecting your career.

Taking the time to define and figure out if what you are feeling is truly love, infatuation, or just an attraction can help you manage the situation better and determine the best ways to handle it. Principles are the behaviors or lifestyles one applies to achieve successful outcomes. When you apply better principles and put them into practice, you find yourself excelling at work while also benefiting from love.

These principles also help in knowing the right time to focus on your job and the right time for love. Research has shown that when workers fall in love with each other, their work attitudes change. If not handled carefully, this can affect their job performance. The truth about life is that we are often carried away by things that give us pleasure, especially love, rather than focusing on what we need to do.

Despite numerous successes and promotions, falling in love and its attractions at the workplace can undermine long-term success if principles are not properly applied. There is nothing wrong with being in love with a co-worker, but it becomes problematic if the love damages or destroys your job success and career.

One thing that should always be at the forefront of your mind is the purpose of your work. Anything that deviates from this purpose needs to be handled wisely. Identifying and applying good principles, and managing love appropriately, will help in promoting confidence in your job while being in love with your co-worker can be positive.

There are many instances of workers who found their spouses at the workplace. These relationships succeeded because the individuals involved applied good principles, understood, and maintained boundaries between their job and their love life.

This balance helped them to excel in their job duties while nurturing their relationships.

On the other hand, there are also cases where co-workers who fell in love and got married ended up negatively affecting their job careers, resulting in demotion or termination. This often happens due to a lack of principles and boundaries between work and love.

Also, if you notice a co-worker of the opposite sex trying to seduce you or take advantage of you, applying good principles can help control the situation and maintain your composure.

ASSISTING CO-WORKER'S

One funny aspect about co-workers is how they always love having colleagues do their job for them. It usually starts with a request like, "Please, can you help me with my job? I won't be around for an hour." They are quick to show you how to do their tasks, so you can help them when they are not around. Over time, they start dropping their tasks for you to do, even when they are present, assuming you will handle it for them. Gradually, these tasks become part of your job.

I had a similar experience at one of my previous workplaces. The man in charge of the generator, the generator operator, asked me to switch over to the Nigeria Electricity Power Authority (NEPA) power and switch off the generator whenever the NEPA power was restored, usually when he was not around. I complied and started helping him as a co-worker. However, one day when the NEPA power was restored and he was around, I expected him to do his job. To my surprise, he walked up to me angrily and asked why I hadn't switched over the power. He even questioned if I couldn't observe that the NEPA power had been restored.

I responded with anger, saying, "I was only helping when you weren't around. Why are you shouting at me? Is it part of my job?" He kept quiet and walked away. From that moment on, I stopped helping him with the light switching.

You should be very careful about how you help your co-workers with their tasks. When this help starts to become an opportunity for them to take advantage of you, quickly put a stop to it with a firm response if needed. Otherwise, you will end up doing their jobs, making your workload cumbersome while they do nothing.

CHAPTER THREE

JOB, FASHION AND SOCIAL LIFE STYLE

Fashion and social lifestyles have been challenges for workers in various subtle ways. Many companies impose strict rules and regulations on their employees' fashion choices and personal lifestyles, which deprive workers of their self-expression and freedom. These restrictions can include prohibitions on using cell phones while at work, bans on social discussions except those related to the job, specific dress codes and color schemes dictated by the company, and restrictions on hairstyles and traditional attire as determined by bosses and company policies. These constraints often cause emotional distress among workers.

I experienced this firsthand at one of my previous workplaces. We were not allowed to use phones while working or talk to each other unless it was work-related. Social gatherings, even during breaks, were prohibited unless they took place outside the company premises, where workers could be themselves. Although the job was not particularly difficult and the salary was manageable, the lack of freedom was extremely challenging for all workers. We felt like prisoners in the middle of our job.

Gradually, many of us began falling ill one after another, which seemed almost magical. As a result, many found it difficult to cope with the company's rules and decisions. Slowly, we started quitting one by one, prioritizing our freedom and health over working in such a tyrannical environment. Despite needing the job, it was better to avoid emotional instability and health deficiencies. It is good for workers to be in an environment where they can feel free and express themselves.

LIFESTYLES AND DRESSING

Lifestyles, dressing, and fashion are personal expressions of freedom for workers and often reflect their happiness and uniqueness. These styles showcase the level of social influence workers have, but in some cases, jobs impose specific styles that may not align with workers' passions. Some employers dictate workers' hairstyles, clothing, patterns, colors, dress codes, and even behaviors such as restricting social discussions and cell phone usage during work hours. This imposition can lead to emotional distress among workers.

During my time at a distributor's company, the boss always emphasized the importance of dressing to uphold the company's good image. However, I expressed concern that such standards were not reflected in my salary. I emphasized that what I was paid could not cover the cost of such attire. While I am not against dressing well, I believe companies should not demand high fashion standards without adequately compensating employees.

Some bosses expect high standards of dressing while paying low salaries, hoping for a magical transformation in appearance. In such cases, it is crucial for companies to reflect these standards in workers' salaries. However, workers should be cautious not to overshoot their dressing and fashion styles beyond their means, as it could lead to assumptions of misconduct or theft by the company.

Expressing oneself through fashion choices can sometimes act as a barrier to job opportunities. Tattoos, dress patterns, hairstyles, and nail grooming should be carefully considered to avoid negative perceptions in the workplace.

Competing with co-workers on fashion rather than job performance is detrimental. While fashion can boost confidence and enhance job performance, it should not overshadow job responsibilities. Workers should view fashion as a personal expression rather than a competition. Dressing appropriately can create a positive environment and enhance client interactions.

Some organizations enforce a corporate dress code without specifying fashion choices. In such cases, workers should dress according to their job position. Dressing too low or too high compared to one's position can affect one's respect level among co-workers and may prompt negative reactions from the boss.

I recall an incident from my time as a driver when I dressed above my position. While my boss initially approved, he later stopped giving me the usual token of appreciation. Perhaps he perceived my attire as a sign of additional income. Dressing well can draw positive attention, but dressing above one's position may unintentionally create competition and tension with the boss.

In cases where one feels marginalized, stepping up in clothing and lifestyle may be necessary to regain respect and position within the organization.

SOCIAL ACTIVITIES

Both workers and companies should prioritize promoting social lifestyle activities among coworkers, friends, and family. These activities foster team bonding, social outings, annual parties, and recognition of workers' invitations with a good track record of participation.

TEAM BONDING

Team bonding involves organizing social activities within departments or teams to engage in stress-free fun. These events aim to relieve tensions and heal any conflicts that may have arisen during work transactions. Sponsored by team members or the company, these activities are exclusive to the department or team. They provide an opportunity for members to choose a day and location, such as a beach party, memorable restaurant, museum, or virtual gathering, to rejuvenate and motivate the team.

SOCIAL OUTING

Social outings involve gatherings with associates, friends, and family for recreational purposes. These outings may include playing games, sports, stand-up comedy, or creating family-oriented activities. Such outings provide workers with a chance to unwind and release stress accumulated from work. Engaging in playful activities with family members helps workers rejuvenate and reconnect with family values, fostering a sense of responsibility and readiness for work.

ANNUAL PARTY

Annual parties, typically held at the end of the year, are organized and funded by companies to celebrate achievements and appreciate workers' contributions. These events are filled with fun activities, awards, and commendations, aiming to strengthen the bond among workers and recognize their efforts in achieving company goals. Annual parties serve as a platform to connect workers and motivate them to strive for further success in the upcoming year.

COLLEAGUES INVITATIONS

Workers often extend invitations to their coworkers and company to be a part of their personal milestones, such as birthdays, weddings, or during times of mourning. Participating in these events fosters a sense of camaraderie and loyalty among coworkers. Companies and coworkers' involvement in workers' personal lives through recognizing and honoring invitations not only boosts morale but also encourages workers to remain emotionally stable and committed to their job responsibilities.

Encouraging and facilitating these social lifestyle activities within the workplace not only enhances team dynamics but also contributes to a positive work environment and overall job satisfaction.

CHAPTER FOUR

THE EFFECTS AND PAIN BEHIND JOB SUCCESS

One of the issues confronting both workers and retirees is the pain derived from their jobs. Jobs are intended to provide livelihood, encouragement, and positive memories, yet sometimes they inflict pain and negative feelings on workers, leading to challenges and emotional disturbances during and after employment.

JOB AND THEIR EFFECTS

Employment enables individuals to afford their daily needs and aspire to a comfortable or even luxurious lifestyle. Undoubtedly, jobs play a crucial role in supporting humanity. However, there are aspects of jobs that can be detrimental to human well-being, including mental stress, physical ailments, and the development of negative habits.

It is imperative to recognize the adverse effects of certain job-related factors on human health. By understanding and addressing these deficiencies, individuals can mitigate the negative impact of their work on their well-being both during and after their employment. Failure to do so may result in individuals carrying the burden of past job-related trauma, which can pose significant risks to their health and interpersonal relationships in their present lives.

Many individuals find it challenging to detach from their past jobs, often carrying with them both mental and physical characteristics long after leaving their positions. Unfortunately, this can lead to dehumanizing behavior towards others and self-harm.

Some jobs, initially intended to be beneficial, can become problematic due to the handicaps they impose on workers during duty. Accidents involving toxic or sharp objects may result in disabilities or amputations, causing mental and physical distress and character deficiencies. Consequently, many workers suffer, sometimes to the extent of contemplating suicide, especially when compensation from companies is inadequate or non-existent.

Moreover, the work environment and practices, influenced by commands, orders, and societal norms, can degrade workers' dignity and impact their behavior even after leaving their jobs. It's crucial for workers to recognize and manage these negative influences through rehabilitation techniques to prevent harming themselves and others post-employment.

Reflecting on a personal experience as a field operational driver, encountering road rage among drivers highlighted the detrimental effects of negative societal influences. Engaging in confrontations and insults not only hurt each other but also negatively impacted bystanders, including children, perpetuating a cycle of aggression and intimidation.

In workplaces where dishonesty is encouraged, employees may become desensitized to lying, affecting their integrity in personal relationships. It's essential to address and rehabilitate such behaviors to maintain personal values and trustworthiness.

Workers should proactively save and invest in rehabilitation to address any negative influences from their jobs, ensuring their well-being and preventing harm to themselves and others in the future.

JOB PAIN

Job pains encompass the emotional toll and stress endured during and after employment, often haunting workers long after they have left their jobs. These pains may stem from injuries sustained during service, resulting in disability and economic hardship. Additionally, they can arise from a sense of unfulfilled dreams and aspirations, where years of dedicated work seem to amount to nothing upon retirement.

Workers may experience job pains as a result of achieving career success through ethically questionable means, such as harming colleagues or engaging in deceitful practices. These actions may lead to feelings of remorse and sadness later in life, tarnishing the memories of one's career achievements.

Life is a collection of memories, and as workers approach retirement age, they often find themselves reflecting on how they spent their years in the workforce. This introspection may be fueled by fears of mortality or a loss of control over one's life. For some, this reflection brings about a sense of regret and longing to rectify past wrongs, even though such actions are irreversible.

Retirement should ideally be a time of joy and fulfillment, free from the burdens of job-related pains. However, for many, the lingering regrets and sorrows associated with their career choices can cast a shadow over this period of life transition.

CHAPTER FIVE

JOBS, AGE AND GENDER CONTRADITIONS IN NIGERIA CULTURES AND BELIEFS

Age and gender differences present challenges in the workplace, often leading to emotional disturbances and conflicts if not managed effectively by both workers and management. While industries prioritize competence and leadership qualities in their authoritative staff, regardless of age or gender, the dynamics within teams can sometimes lead to tension and discord among workers.

In many industries, age and gender are considered irrelevant when selecting leaders, as companies prioritize individuals who can effectively advance the company's interests. However, this approach may clash with traditional African cultural norms, where age and gender often determine authority, with older individuals typically assuming leadership roles.

In today's world, experience and qualifications often take precedence over age and gender, particularly in Western societies driven by capitalism. This shift in priorities has led to a divergence from traditional African beliefs regarding leadership and authority.

The disconnect between industry practices and African cultural norms has resulted in conflicts and challenges for individuals who find themselves caught between these two worlds. While modern Africa is gradually embracing industry standards, the pain of disregarding traditional values continues to impact African workers in various ways.

It's crucial for both workers and management to navigate these differences sensitively, acknowledging the cultural context while also recognizing the importance of competence and meritocracy in achieving organizational goals.

This story reminds me of a boss I once worked with, a younger woman who, despite our African cultural norms that emphasize respect for elders, demanded to be addressed with authority and respect according to company policy. We were instructed to follow her lead and address her as "ma," without regard for traditional African values. When we eventually parted ways, we unexpectedly crossed paths again. As she called me by name, I reciprocated by addressing her directly. To my surprise, she appeared embarrassed and angered by my actions, seemingly interpreting them as disrespect.

Reflecting on this encounter, I pondered whether she had forsaken her African heritage by refusing to acknowledge traditional cultural norms of respect for elders. It struck me that as leaders, we should strive not to assert our age over others, but rather to foster cooperation and mutual respect among team members while guiding them toward their goals.

Despite efforts by some companies to address this issue by implementing policies that discourage the use of formal titles like "Mr." or "Mrs., Sir and Ma" and promote a more casual approach of addressing each other by name, achieving a balance remains elusive. Industries are driven by their objectives and are often reluctant to adopt practices that might conflict with their goals. As workers, navigating this balance requires us to consider both the cultural values of our society, particularly in Nigeria and Africa, and the ethical standards and objectives of our workplaces.

Finding this balance involves applying authority in a manner that respects cultural traditions while also upholding the values and goals of the company. By acknowledging and integrating both sets of values, workers can strive for success without compromising their cultural identity or professional integrity.

CHAPTER SIX

JOB MISSION AND VISION

Job missions and visions can pose significant challenges to workers who join a company without clearly understanding their own purpose and the company's objectives. Workers who lack alignment between their personal goals and the company's mission and vision often struggle to find fulfillment and may experience emotional distress and unfulfilled dreams. To address this issue, many companies organize seminars and invite career experts to help shape workers' understanding of both individual and company goals, fostering a win-win environment.

COMPANY'S VISION AND MISSION

A company's mission encompasses the specific methods, steps, and processes that guide workers in achieving the company's goals and purposes. The vision, on the other hand, represents the aspirational and future-oriented objectives the company hopes to achieve.

SELF VISION AND MISSION

Every organization operates with a mission and vision. For workers, it is crucial to develop a personal mission and vision that align with the company's goals, particularly within their specific department or role. This alignment helps workers stand out and contribute meaningfully to the organization.

Personal vision and mission involve unique approaches and transformative practices that workers apply to support the company's objectives. This can include going above and beyond in client interactions, offering solutions, or dedicating extra time to enhance the company's success.

Practicing a self-vision and mission aligned with the company's goals helps workers prepare and adapt, fostering a sense of purpose and accomplishment. Over time, these practices become ingrained, showcasing the worker's strengths and adding value during performance appraisals.

SELF CAREER VISION AND MISSION

Just as companies have their vision and mission, workers should have their own as well. Having a self-vision and mission before starting any job is crucial. These personal goals serve as a guideline for achieving a better future and purpose. A worker's self-vision should encompass how they see themselves and what they aspire to become, considering how the company can assist in this career-building process.

A worker's self-vision is the imagined future they hope to accomplish, while their mission consists of the steps and actions taken to reach these goals. These steps might include maintaining a positive attitude, humility, loyalty, integrity, determination, focus, confidence, respect, good rationale, and a strong work ethic.

The mission to achieve one's vision can start with seemingly small or common tasks, with the hope of eventual elevation to a dream job and career. For some, this might involve spending many productive years with a company to reach their career aspirations.

To illustrate, think of vision as what you see when you look at a distant object, and mission as the focused effort needed to reach it. Just as a blink can make you lose sight of that object, losing focus on your mission can hinder achieving your vision.

CHAPTER SEVEN

JOB AND RELIGION

Religion has been a major challenge for workers and companies, affecting job performance through the habits and beliefs of employees. The inability of government and religious leaders to control and correct workers' mindsets has created significant differences in the workplace. In some cases, a worker's religion may determine whether they get a job or not. It is important to be careful when interacting with coworkers to avoid conflicts with their beliefs. For example, some religious practices do not allow their female members to shake hands with men. Unknowingly offering a handshake can offend them. Some religions also restrict women's participation in the workforce, creating emotional disturbances and differences among workers.

RELIGION

Religion is crucial in Nigeria and must be handled carefully in relation to jobs. It affects job opportunities, with different religious beliefs and practices often clashing in the workplace. Workers must learn to manage their religious behavior at work to avoid causing problems, recognizing that religion is a personal matter. While religion can help restrain bad working attitudes and decision-making, it can also cause conflict when one religion's practices are seen as offensive to another.

Some companies believe in unifying religious practices, such as holding morning devotions that all workers must attend. This can create feelings of betrayal and loss of interest in the job among workers whose beliefs are different. For example, a Christian worker might feel uncomfortable participating in a morning devotion led in a Muslim manner, or a Muslim woman might feel offended by being asked to shake hands with male coworkers.

I once heard from a Christian colleague who shared his experience working for a company where the boss imposed fasting and prayer sessions without explaining their purpose. This colleague had eaten before coming to work, and during the prayer session, the boss singled him out for not fasting. Later, the boss insisted he take part in a communion service with bread and malt drinks, which contradicted his religious beliefs. Refusing to participate led to conflict and eventually cost him his job.

A similar situation happened to me in Lagos. I was asked to lead a prayer during a weekly devotion, and my prayer style differed from that of my coworkers. Afterward, a colleague asked about my church, and I explained that our prayers end with everyone saying "amen" together, unlike their continuous "amen." This difference led to ongoing explanations to my coworkers, highlighting the need for mutual respect.

The best way to manage job and religious differences is by respecting others' beliefs. Respect fosters peace and good relationships in the workplace, even if you don't share the same beliefs. Criticizing or condemning coworkers based on their religion can damage relationships and create conflict. Instead, preach your beliefs without attacking others' practices.

When asked to do something that contradicts your religious beliefs, politely explain that you respect their practices but cannot participate due to your own beliefs. In well-organized companies, this approach should be respected, and policies should accommodate all workers.

It is essential to address situations where bosses or company owners try to control workers' faith and religious beliefs due to their authority. Workers should assert their right to religious freedom respectfully and seek policies that ensure everyone's beliefs are respected.

CHAPTER EIGHT

RANKS AND SETTINGS IN THE ORGANIZATION

Job ranking and settings have been major problems within companies, where benefits, bonuses, and job grades differ, leaving some workers without entitlements. This disparity causes workers to lose interest and slow down their job performance, feeling it's unfair to do more work for less or no benefits.

MANAGEMENT STAFF

These workers are highly qualified and have the rights and privileges to analyze, bargain, determine, and influence company decisions and policies as board members. They play a crucial role in shaping the company's future through their ideas and initiatives. Management staff members act as intermediaries between the general workers and company directors. Their positions allow them to make critical decisions that affect the entire company. They are often seen as the company's backbone, ensuring that everything runs smoothly and efficiently.

STAFF WORKERS

These workers are qualified and recognized by the company to receive most working benefits and rights but are not part of the decision-making process unless promoted to managerial positions. They often feel that management staff trade off workers' rights, gains, and freedoms for their own financial benefits and promotions. Company staff workers can be quickly dismissed or set up if they do not show loyalty or do not follow management's directions. Despite this, they are the core workforce, responsible for the day-to-day operations that keep the company running.

OUTSOURCED STAFF WORKERS

These workers are hired through third-party agencies and are not directly employed by the company they work for. Their rights, salaries, and benefits are limited due to third-party involvement. They are vulnerable to being dismissed for any mistakes and rarely get promotions. Outsourcing staff are often sidelined and intimidated by other workers, such as management and company staff, because they are not recognized as part of the company's direct staff. Their identification cards clearly show the name of the outsourcing company, distinguishing them from other employees. This creates a sense of alienation and inferiority among them, impacting their morale and productivity.

CONTRACT WORKERS

These workers have annual or biannual contracts with plans for renewal based on performance. They have limited benefits and are not recognized by board directors. Their ID cards are marked with validation dates. Contract workers face high risks due to minimal medical entitlements and can be pushed to over-deliver without proper care. This type of employment is often seen as a way for companies to manage labor costs while avoiding long-term commitments. Contract workers are in a constant state of uncertainty, as their employment is contingent on periodic reviews and renewals, making it difficult for them to plan for the future.

CASUAL WORKERS

These workers have no appointment letters, entitlements, or identification linking them to the company. They are paid daily or weekly wages based on hours worked. Casual workers, known as "survival of the fittest," carry the highest risks with no recognition or security from the company and can be replaced at any moment. They often perform the most physically demanding and least rewarding jobs. Casual workers have no job security, benefits, or health coverage, leaving them vulnerable to exploitation and abuse. Their hope for a stable future relies heavily on their daily performance and the mercy of their employers.

In many parts of Africa, including Nigeria, companies have taken advantage of the economic situation to employ workers under these precarious conditions. This system allows companies to reduce labor costs significantly, but it comes at the expense of workers' welfare and job satisfaction. The lack of fair compensation, job security, and benefits leads to a demoralized workforce, which ultimately affects the company's overall productivity and reputation.

For companies to thrive and maintain a motivated workforce, they need to address these disparities in job ranking and settings. Providing fair compensation, job security, and benefits to all categories of workers can lead to a more dedicated and productive workforce. This approach not only benefits the workers but also enhances the company's reputation and success in the long run.

CHAPTER NINE

JOB AND PAY

Salary and pay can create problems for workers when the value of their services is undermined. In such cases, workers are paid very low wages compared to their contributions to the company. Even if workers are passionate about their jobs, inadequate salaries and wages become a problem. This issue affects their passion and enthusiasm for creating, developing, and researching ideas that could help achieve company goals. It's clear that insufficient monetary compensation for their services is a major challenge, making it difficult for workers to cope with daily life. Low pay discourages workers and diminishes their motivation and eagerness to excel.

SALARIES AND WAGES

Salaries and wages have different meanings. Today, a few workers are paid salaries while many are paid wages instead, especially in Nigeria, where wages are gradually replacing salaries. A salary is a fixed amount of money paid to workers, usually measured on a monthly or annual basis, including components like basic salary, house allowance, transport allowance, meal allowance, utility allowance, etc., to derive the gross salary. Wages refer to a worker's total income for a specific time period.

Workers often wonder why some are paid more than others. The differences in pay are based on various factors such as workers' experiences, years with the company, educational background, and the company's growth and development.

Other factors include the labor market, government policies, skills, educational value, and risk evaluation.

The wrong method of salary payment is often a major job problem in Nigeria and Africa. Companies' payment patterns can be worrisome to workers, leading many job seekers to scrutinize the payment system before applying. Companies often use these irregular payment methods to prevent workers from quitting easily, claiming to have their own calendar different from the normal one. Workers' agitations on this issue have repeatedly failed, and the government's inability to intervene in the labor market has left workers with no hope but divine intervention. This method of salary payment causes significant damage to workers' budgeting and spending, making it difficult to achieve their monthly or annual goals.

UNDERPAID SALARIES

Underpayment of salary occurs when workers are not paid fairly for their services. This results from industries taking advantage of workers in the labor market and governmental influences, such as an oversupply of laborers and policies that encourage slave labor. The government's failure to implement good policies allows employers to hire cheap labor and exploit workers. Companies justify underpayment by blaming the government for multiple taxes, tariffs, and levies, arguing that fiscal policies do not consider citizens' well-being.

In summary, salary and wage issues are significant problems for workers, affecting their motivation and overall life. Proper compensation and payment methods are crucial for maintaining worker satisfaction and productivity.

SUB-CHARGES OF SALARY

Sub-charging of salary refers to methods companies use to deduct workers' salaries as a result of disciplinary actions, such as charges for lateness, reduction for time not worked, damages incurred, and more. This means that when workers are performing their job duties, any risks associated with the job have been analyzed and internalized to be borne by the workers through these salary deductions. This practice affects workers' net pay and take-home salaries, often making them less productive. These deductions, while intended to enforce discipline, end up demotivating workers, as they feel their efforts are not fairly compensated. The net effect of these deductions is often a decrease in workers' overall productivity and morale.

INCONVENIENCE ALLOWANCE

These are extra payments added to workers' wages based on the additional services and risks rendered to the company. Workers see these services as a means of increasing their salaries. However, the added responsibilities and extra work often come at the expense of their health and well-being. Companies prefer to overburden existing employees rather than hire additional staff, as this approach is more cost-effective for them. This practice can lead to long-term health challenges for workers. Employees should weigh the value of these extra services against their health and opt for them occasionally rather than as a daily routine. Over time, this can result in significant health issues, which may lead to increased absenteeism and decreased overall productivity.

BUDGET AND PLANNING

Workers' budgeting and planning involve outlining intended expenditures and proposals for how to meet them. As a salary earner, it is crucial to budget and plan your monthly expenses productively. Effective budgeting and planning enable workers to achieve more with their income than they might have imagined. It strengthens the connection between workers and their work purposes, helping them realize career goals and dreams. Without proper planning and budgeting, workers often achieve little. For instance, planning your expenses allows you to allocate funds for necessary expenses, savings, and investments. This ensures that you live within your means and are prepared for any unexpected financial emergencies.

Sometimes, co-workers may want to review your salary budget and expenditures out of curiosity or jealousy, especially if you save more and spend less than they do. This can lead to workplace competition, with some employees spending excessively on food and clothes to keep up with colleagues, ultimately working for years without significant savings or achievements. It's important for workers to have a purpose and target before taking a job, working for reasons, and budgeting to achieve success. Effective budgeting can also help workers identify areas where they can cut costs and save more money. This can lead to increased financial security and peace of mind.

PENSION SERVICES AND REMITTANCE

Pension services and remittance are government-initiated programs to help workers secure their financial future. Companies and employees are required to contribute a percentage of the worker's salary to a pension account. This system was introduced to ensure that workers live comfortably after retirement. However, some companies find it difficult to comply with these remittance policies, often skipping payments despite deducting the required amount from workers' salaries. This non-compliance can jeopardize workers' retirement plans and financial security.

Workers need to educate themselves about their pension accounts, monitoring them just like their bank accounts. Attending seminars, webinars, and making inquiries can help them take advantage of any announcements or benefits from pension insurance companies. Workers should regularly check their pension statements to ensure that the correct contributions are being made and to identify any discrepancies early on. This proactive approach can help workers make informed decisions about their retirement planning and ensure they are on track to meet their retirement goals.

CONSUMPTION AND SAVINGS

Workers often fail to understand that their jobs influence their consumption choices and savings. Co-workers' attitudes can significantly affect one's spending and saving habits. Initially, a worker might plan to save a certain percentage of their salary, but over time, the influence of co-workers can derail this plan. This influence can come in the form of peer pressure to spend on non-essential items or to participate in costly social activities.

Maintaining good relationships with co-workers is important, but not at the expense of letting them control your consumption habits. For instance, co-workers may pressure you to buy goods on credit or spend excessively on food, which can affect your savings. Prudent workers must be principled and confident to resist such influences and stay focused on their financial goals.

It's important to establish and stick to a budget that aligns with your financial goals and priorities. This can help you avoid unnecessary expenses and ensure that you are saving and investing enough for the future.

I recall a situation where my co-workers wanted me to purchase goods on credit alongside them. When I declined, it generated tension, and they criticized me. Despite explaining that I had budget my salary, they didn't understand, making me feel awkward. Some workers even sell products at the workplace, expecting everyone to buy them, and leading to conflicts if you refuse. This can create a hostile work environment and make it difficult for you to stick to your financial goals.

Your level of consumption determines your savings. For example, if you spend 70% of your salary on goods and food, you save only 30%. Co-workers often influence spending habits, making it challenging to save. I remember being mocked for having a simple lunch, but I stayed firm in my budgeting plans. Eventually, my colleagues admired my achievements, realizing the importance of budgeting and planning. Despite initial challenges, I maintained my financial discipline and left the organization as a focused and successful person. This experience taught me the importance of staying true to my financial goals and not letting external influences derail my plans.

JOINT CONSUMABLE GOODS

Joint goods are consumable items and foods uniformly consumed by workers from a company, such as televisions, air conditioners, drinks, meals, clothes, chairs, etc. These items and goods are often provided freely by companies to enhance worker productivity and efficiency. Workers have observed that companies sometimes provide goods, meals, and tea daily, weekly, or occasionally to appreciate their efforts, enhance their abilities, and ensure they perform their jobs in good health. Such provisions might include morning tea, free drinking water, or lunch, aimed at keeping workers energetic, strong, and fit for their jobs.

However, there can be negative consequences when workers start noticing negative attitudes and energy from their colleagues. For example, when free water is provided for all workers and visitors, some workers may become judgmental when others fetch water. They might complain that someone is consuming more than their share or criticize the way they fetch it. Similarly, going for morning coffee might attract negative looks, suggesting that is all the worker cares about.

This negativity often stems from a mindset where some workers feel they should be the ones to have it all. This can cause worry and stress, making one feels like they can't exist without these provisions. Gradually, this can affect their career relationships and thinking, leading to a loss of respect from colleagues.

In life, there are many things workers need to give up, not because they are weak, but because they want to be stronger and wiser, fostering a good atmosphere that enables better job performance. Although these consumable goods are intended for good, the negative attitudes of some workers toward them cause problems, making others less inclined to consume these goods frequently.

Choosing to forgo some of these provisions, which cost nothing financially, can help maintain peace and respect. For instance, bringing your own filled water bottle to work or purchasing your own supplies can reduce the tension and necessity of relying on company provisions. Avoid pushing too hard to access these items and, if possible, let go sometimes. Doing this will help create an enabling environment for you to perform your job well and build good relationships with negative co-workers.

FREE JOB SERVICES, CHARITY, AND SELF-PAY

The truth about people in the labor industry or doing what they do to earn a living tells a lot about responsibilities and remuneration. Beyond personal and family responsibilities, there is an inherent responsibility to care for the earth and nature, regardless of one's job or income. I always encourage workers to pave the way for future generations and contribute to their share of earthly and natural duties. By doing so, it eases their freedom and enhances their sense of being.

Free job services are tasks workers perform without negotiation or payment. These are occasional efforts added to their regular duties without the company's awareness. I call this appreciation service; it generates personal passion, reduces the burden of natural responsibilities, and draws blessings. Such services should come from the worker's heart and be chosen freely, without the company's consent. This might include extra time, gifts, or additional effort spent occasionally. However, these acts should not be taken advantage of by the boss and must be done without their knowledge. These services should not contradict company policies or create issues among co-workers. They should align with the company's mission and be delivered with good intentions.

Collective efforts among co-workers can also express gratitude to the company, but this approach may not achieve its full purpose. Some workers may not be emotionally connected to the cause, which is meant to be a heartfelt wish to mother earth, seeking blessings and easing natural tensions.

Charity involves benevolence, humanity, kindness, and goodwill toward the poor and suffering, carried out through activities or gifts benefiting those in needs. Workers engaging in charity answer the call of the earth and contribute to building a better world, attracting blessings, encouraging others, and fostering a good environment. Life is about giving and receiving, but charity from the heart attracts many favors. Workers should not only focus on receiving pay but also on giving time and tokens to the needy, such as the disabled, impoverished, and sick. Giving, even when one is lacking, helps tackle unseen circumstances and fosters a sense of humanity.

Charity should be a voluntary act from a good heart, not one that makes you feel worthless. To achieve this, workers should plan how to participate in charitable activities, whether through monthly donations of 2-5% of their salary or roadside gifts to the homeless and disabled. By giving to those less fortunate, workers connect with the earth, achieving natural happiness regardless of future circumstances.

Self-pay is the small amount workers set aside from their salary each month to satisfy personal cravings and desires. Workers often have unfulfilled needs between paychecks due to financial constraints, but setting aside a small percentage of their salary, such as 2-3%, can make them feel happy and renewed. This practice does not hinder taking care of responsibilities but keeps workers hopeful and energetic. Many workers lose self-happiness by not satisfying their desires, feeling too weak to handle responsibilities. Low salary should not be an excuse to avoid self-pay, and it should not require a high budget.

Self-pay on meals refers to enjoying food or restaurants that bring joy and uplift the spirit, reviving hope and dreams. Self-pay on gifts involves purchasing items that provide worth and a sense of achievement. Achieving self-pay on material items can be challenging for low-income earners, but it is possible by saving a small percentage of their salary over two to three months.

CHAPTER TEN

JOB AND STRENGTH

Job strength can be very challenging for workers who underestimate the little things they can do to boost and gain more strength, as well as create a good atmosphere that will assist them in carrying out their duties effectively. This, in turn, will produce good energy and results, helping them to stand out.

Working strength is the combination of ability and wisdom behind a worker's success at work. Some workers believe that physical body strength is the sole determinant of their success. Of course, working strength is a significant factor. Physical attributes like body weight, height, and facial appearance are important. However, many workers fail to consider the importance of mental and character strengths as crucial tools for standing out at work.

Yes, there are some jobs that demand physical fitness, such as security roles, policing, bodyguard services, construction jobs, and more. These roles require good physical strength and fitness. Yet, character and wisdom are equally necessary to excel in these jobs. Workers who believe that greatness at work relies solely on high physical body strength, without valuing mental and character strengths, limit their potential for greatness. This mindset has led many workers with less physical strength to be held back and afraid of taking on certain jobs. Some even go as far as consuming hard drugs to match the physical strength demands, aiming to be fit for the job.

While physical attributes are vital in certain roles, if your natural body strength and structure do not meet these demands, it's essential to seek jobs that align better with your physical capabilities. Despite physical body advantages, workers still need mental agility and good character to perform their duties diligently and become extraordinary in their roles.

There are many ways and abilities to build strength that worker might not consider which can make them extraordinary and unique. These strengths are not necessarily physical but are related to mental and character development. Through learning and practice, these attributes can significantly enhance a worker's performance and effectiveness on the job. For instance, improving time management skills, developing emotional intelligence, fostering a positive attitude, and enhancing problem-solving abilities are all mental and character-based strengths that can help workers excel.

Additionally, continuous learning and professional development can provide workers with new skills and knowledge, further enhancing their job performance. Building strong relationships with colleagues and supervisors can create a supportive work environment, boosting morale and productivity. Workers should also prioritize their mental health and well-being, ensuring they are mentally fit to handle job challenges.

While physical strength is important in certain jobs, mental and character strengths are equally vital. By focusing on developing these attributes, workers can enhance their job performance, stand out in their roles, and achieve greater success in their careers.

TIME

Time is a crucial factor in every aspect of human life, from sleeping and eating to working. There is a time for everything, and how we manage it can significantly impact our success. At work, time management determines the results we bring home, yet many workers overlook time as a strength. Your effectiveness in using time directly correlates with your job performance. Regardless of how skilled or knowledgeable you are, poor time management can undermine your potential.

Workers often adhere strictly to official start and end times; not realizing that adding a little extra time can make a significant difference. Arriving early and staying a bit later can demonstrate dedication and seriousness, setting you apart from your peers. This commitment can lead to recognition and career advancement. Unfortunately, many workers focus solely on the prescribed hours, missing opportunities to excel.

For example, when I worked at a private hospital in Nigeria as a driver, my official start time was eight o'clock in the morning. However, I chose to arrive at seven o'clock every day. Initially, it was challenging to wake up at five o'clock and prepare, but I persisted because I knew it would help me stand out. Over time, this habit became part of my routine, and my punctuality was noticed. Colleagues often asked how I managed to be so consistent, even after late nights. My dedication paid off when I received an award for being the most punctual worker of the year.

Effective time management is not just about punctuality; it's about using your time wisely throughout the day. For instance, in factory jobs where workers share collective time schedules, arriving early can still be beneficial. Even if you can't start working immediately, being present and prepared before your shift begins demonstrates reliability and commitment. This can enhance your reputation and open doors for future opportunities.

Time management also involves planning for unforeseen circumstances. Many workers aim to leave home just in time to reach work, but this leaves no room for unexpected delays like traffic. By planning to arrive early, you account for these possibilities and reduce the risk of being late. This proactive approach shows foresight and responsibility, qualities that are highly valued in any workplace.

The sacrifice required for good time management can be significant, but the rewards are worth it. Success often involves enduring some difficulties, and effective time management is no exception. It reflects your relationship with your job and your level of commitment. Consistently managing your time well can lead to better job retention and career progression.

Time management is a vital skill that can greatly influence your work performance and career trajectory. By prioritizing time, arriving early, and planning for the unexpected, you can demonstrate dedication and reliability. These qualities not only help you stand out but also build a strong foundation for long-term success. Recognizing the importance of time and managing it effectively is crucial for any worker aiming to excel in their career.

PUNCTUALITY

Punctuality is the state of a worker being present when needed at the exact time of an engagement; it is also a habit of adhering to an appointed time. Punctuality is one of the greatest job strengths workers often overlook. Being punctual at work is not just about waiting for the time to be announced before making yourself available; it involves understanding the nature of your job, knowing, calculating, and predicting when and where you might be needed. The power of punctuality cannot be underestimated; it reflects the strength and willingness of workers to succeed in their roles.

Punctuality helps in expanding a worker's experience and creates opportunities to grow and learn other fields as a result of the unavailability of other workers at critical times. This makes the available worker indispensable. Workers' punctuality should be practiced on fair grounds, ensuring it does not jeopardize their co-workers' jobs.

FOCUS AND PERSISTENCE

Your focus is your direction while your direction is your thinking and your thinking is your thought while persistence is the forces of continuity toward your focus and direction despite the pains along the line with the mindset of achieving end results or goals.

Focusing on your job demands a high rate of effort. The outcome of your delivery is quantified by the level of your focus on your job. Some workers believe in focusing only within working hours but don't realize that great thoughts about job focus often occur outside those hours. These insights might come while relaxing at night or early in the morning. The more you consider your job as your top priority, the more effort you will put into increasing your focus. Your job thoughts should accompany you everywhere, provided the environment is conducive for thinking.

One of the best times for workers to think about job success is first thing in the morning while still in bed. Wake up earlier and spend twenty minutes thinking about your job success, how to be persistent, and ways to deliver quality work. Reflect on what went wrong the previous day, where you could have persisted more for better results, and learn to appraise yourself on the previous day's tasks. Your persistence and focus help find solutions to job challenges and introduce techniques and methods to achieve the best results.

Challenges that can affect your focus and persistence include your salary. If workers are underpaid, it can create reasons not to be highly focused and can slow persistence toward job success. Do not let salary issues disturb your focus. Provided you have defined goals on the job, such as knowing when to move on or viewing the job as training for a better-paying opportunity, the training will make you strong and unique, allowing you to stand out in a new job when the opportunity arises.

The social life workers engage in can determine the level of focus they give to their job. Be mindful of the kind of social activities you participate in. Many social environments that workers get involved in might deprive them of high focus and persistence on their job. Any social activity that doesn't promote or encourage your job will likely detract from your focus and persistence.

You also need to balance your focus and persistence with family life. If not balanced with family, it can become a problem and affect your thinking and focus. Balancing your job with family provides the foundation for maintaining focus and persistence, giving workers the grace and freedom to be happy with their job.

It is crucial to strike a balance between work and personal life to maintain a high level of focus and persistence. Remember, achieving this balance not only contributes to job success but also ensures personal happiness and well-being. Therefore, cultivate habits that enhance your focus and persistence, while also nurturing your personal life and relationships. This approach will lead to a more fulfilling career and life.

PASSION

The motive behind work is driven by passion and rewards, such as high pay. Without proper motivation, workers lose interest, leading to decreased job satisfaction in the long run. An unmotivated job can negatively affect workers emotionally, mentally, and physically, impacting their performance and well-being.

Monetary rewards alone do not guarantee long-term motivation if workers lack passion. This inner discontent often pushes them to seek freedom and liberation. True liberation comes when workers engage in jobs they enjoy, without regrets about the risks and pay, as long as there is passion and career fulfillment.

Lack of job security forces many to remain in unfulfilling jobs, causing lasting pain from not achieving career freedom or job passion. However, unfulfilling jobs can serve as stepping stones to more rewarding careers by providing valuable experience and skills. Financial savings from these jobs can be used to advance one's career through further education and skill acquisition, eventually leading to a dream job.

The strain of working in an unfulfilling job can be detrimental. To avoid long-term harm, consider such jobs temporary and continue searching for more fulfilling work. If the job severely impacts mental or emotional health, it is crucial to quit promptly. Although quitting can be difficult due to financial concerns, remaining in an unfulfilling job only exacerbates mental and emotional strain. Preparing financially and otherwise for a job transition can help ease this process.

Workers fear not finding another job after leaving an unfulfilling one, hindering their pursuit of job freedom. It is essential to plan financially and strategically before seeking a better job. To excel at work, learn to develop a love for the job, even if it lacks passion. Creating a positive attitude towards the job can help sustain employment, build skills, and financial strength, ultimately aiding in the pursuit of a more fulfilling career. Cultivating passion for one's work fosters a positive atmosphere, enhances health, and improves job performance.

GREETNGS AND BEING FRIENDLY

Greetings play an important role in building connections among co-workers and capturing clients' feelings, leading to positive outcomes. They reflect a positive mindset and provide a pathway to form meaningful relationships. The frequency of exchanging greetings with colleagues influences how they perceive you and how supportive they can be in helping you achieve your goals.

Regular greetings can pave the way for colleagues to offer assistance, share valuable work techniques, and provide career information that can be beneficial. Workers often complain about unfriendliness among peers due to a lack of greetings, without considering how a simple greeting can foster goodwill and support. This act can encourage co-workers to cover for each other and offer help during difficult times.

Greetings and friendliness indicate loyalty and respect, making co-workers feel valued. This practice is often seen in senior staff and highly experienced workers who greet others warmly, earning admiration and loyalty from their colleagues. For example, in one of my previous workplaces, the company owner made it a point to greet every worker he encountered, regardless of their position. This habit endeared him to the staff, who appreciated his humility and approachability.

Greeting colleagues also demonstrates a clear and positive mindset, especially during disputes. A simple "good morning" can signal a willingness to resolve conflicts and promote unity and love among workers. It is a wise and practical habit that, with continuous practice, can become an integral part of one's character and lifestyle.

In the workplace, it is important to practice the habit of greeting everyone, not just specific individuals. Extend greetings to all colleagues, visitors, and staff members, regardless of their friendliness. Share your greetings with excitement and genuine interest, and do not be discouraged if some do not respond warmly. Focus on the beauty and strength of this practice, as it can significantly uplift the workplace environment.

LEARNING AND PRACTICING

Learning is very applicable in daily life; there are always new things and skills to learn, and much to add to your knowledge if you have learning and practicing mindset. Senior workers often find it difficult to learn from junior workers, especially when the juniors understand the job better. Despite differences in position, junior workers can quickly learn new technologies and job trends. When willing to share, seniors may find it hard to learn from them. If juniors present new methods to the board or company owner, and the idea is accepted, they often gain recognition and may be promoted ahead of the senior staff. This might have benefited both if seniors had collaborated with juniors, valuing the potential for mutual promotion.

Workers shouldn't feel belittled, regardless of job rank or grade. Valuing learning, even from junior staff, can be strength and increase your future value. The most difficult part of learning is its practical application. Research shows that many can explain and discuss knowledge effectively but lack the practice to implement what they know.

Workers' silence and overlooking minor issues can be strengths. Silence on certain matters or behaviors in organizations can make workers stand out and appear more mature, especially in logical cases.

OBEY THE ORDER

Obey before complain has helped many workers in their job. Whenever an order is given to workers, they should learn to obey before complaining. If workers feel or wish to complain, they should do so in a suggestion manner. If their suggestion is not accepted, they should carry on with the order, even if they know the order might yield low results or would not be best. Producing unsuccessful results after already suggesting a better way allows the superior or boss to acknowledge the suggestion for the next mission. When workers complain often or refuse to carry out the order, it diminishes their strength, even if their complaint is valid. If workers must complain, it should not be at the detriment of their job strength. Obeying before complaining shows loyalty, while suggesting in a respectful manner shows value and respect to the boss.

Sometimes, tests will be set for workers by giving them insufficient resources to complete a job. Instead of complaining, workers should make a suggestion. If the boss insists, they should carry on with the job until the resources are exhausted. Then, they should stop and inform the boss with evidence of the work done so far. Workers should not use personal resources to continue the job unless they are sure their money will be returned. Using personal money is a total loss for workers unless it will be reimbursed. Workers should document where the job stops and wait for resources from the office. This demonstrates transparency and strengthens their career. On the next job, the boss will likely consider their suggestions. Using personal resources for company jobs encourages bosses to assign tasks without adequate resources.

RESPECT

Respect is one of the greatest tools in achieving job strength. When I worked at Standard Life Care Hospital (SLCH), I respected every worker, including the newly employed. I approached co-workers with value because I understood the strength and importance of respect. One day, I had the privilege of discussing with a staff nurse. During our conversation, she mentioned a day they had a meeting with the doctor. Workers were grouped according to their positions, and the doctor asked them to vote for the best workers in their categories. To my surprise, all votes in my category went to me except one. The nurses who voted for me were not in the same job category, but they were given the power to vote that day. My respectful approach and good manners helped me gain their support. Although no awards were given, I felt loved and happy. Sometimes, when job performance is tied among colleagues, manners and character can stand out.

I discovered respect as a tool for strength during my university years when I began to recognize and respect my course mates. In my department, I was always simple, respectful, and a good listener. When I decided to run for a post, I was unopposed. People told me they were not voting for anyone else because they believed I was a good person who could unite others. I won, and since then, I have seen the necessity of using manners to achieve greatness in my career.

Workers often expect their job results to make them stand out. However, in some cases, there can be a tie with a fellow worker, and manners can be the deciding factor. Some companies even allow other departments to select the best workers, and in such cases, your manners count a lot alongside your job results. Therefore, I always encourage workers to maintain good manners and strong job performance to gain an advantage over competitors and achieve recognition.

SPICE UP YOUR STRENGTH

Workers should learn how to spice up their strengths when feeling weak and tired on the job by setting up their minds on things that motivate most and taking a few minutes break to meditate on things or words that elevate and encourage their spirit when feeling weak and tried to derive joy and strength while working, and to cheer up. Probably workers can combine such while still working; it could be singing, listening to music, watching a few minute videos, or flashing back on what inspired workers most. However, and whatever workers are able to do to strengthen themselves through the use of spicing, they should make sure they are not disturbing co-workers sitting close or obstructing co-workers' jobs and the organization as a whole. Never say no to your portfolio task, always give it a try. We all know that tasks can be so crazy and hectic most times but it produces strength at its success.

GOOD HEALTH

Health is crucial in strengthening your unique wisdom to succeed at work. It provides the opportunity to express your uniqueness and excel in your job. Taking care of your health is a worker's responsibility, showcasing how fit and capable you are in performing your job.

However, the high cost of healthcare has discouraged workers from properly taking care of their health. Some workers neglect their health until their conditions prevent them from standing up for the day, leading to sickness and deformity. A worker's greatness on the job and their passion for their career contribute to building good healthy relationships.

Research shows that human capital and healthcare are inseparable, as health greatly impacts human ability. Good health is essential for success in a job career. Maintaining good health enables workers to carry out their daily tasks, giving them freedom and mental clarity to perform and deliver their best. It is advisable for workers to view healthcare as a vital tool for effective job performance. Workers often complain about the high cost of healthcare compared to their salaries or wages, but it is crucial to encourage oneself to stay fit for the job.

CHAPTER ELEVEN

JOB AND SELF-SECURITY

Lack of workers' self-security is also one of the challenging parts for workers. Lacking personal security has caused many workers their salaries, reputations, and pain over what they know nothing about, and some have been imprisoned because of a lack of personal security precautions.

SELF-SECURITY

When people talk about security in the workplace, we often assume it is the concern of the company and not of the workers. However, when a case occurs, the company's security personnel and police officers always say everyone is a suspect, making it every worker's concern. Being self-secure in a company isn't about holding arms or blades but being intelligent and careful.

Security has gone a long way to becoming every worker's business. Failure to be self-security conscious as a worker makes you unprofessional in your career, and if care is not taken, you might lose your job due to a lack of self-security.

Security is an attitude that becomes character when often practiced and gradually becomes part of a worker's routine. A worker's practice is who they are because their official character is their career, and workers are what they produce.

On some occasions at the workplace, you might witness or hear about an item going missing after you or a co-worker left a particular office. If you or your co-worker is called as a suspect for entering the office, your failure to practice self-security can make you guilty of something you know nothing about.

Security is procedure, caution, logic, and safety. There is self-security practices you need to emulate based on your job. It is important to seek your co-workers' consent before going to their desk, no matter how friendly you both are. Also, it is vital to always knock at their office door before entering to seek their attention for your arrival.

When the company tells you to give out some goods or money, always keep evidence or acknowledgment of giving it out. This can be documented (a written note signed by the receiver), a cell phone camera picture, or an eyewitness, as the case may be. Signature and date are also part of security and provide accurate information to the parties, settling any improper insinuation, which keeps you both professional and protected.

Security is the wisdom to know the right time to walk out of a particular place, especially where valuable properties are kept, even when trusted, provided you weren't assigned to be there at the moment. The importance of being self-secure, despite the company having its security personnel, is that it keeps you safer; more secure, and out of trouble, either set up or otherwise. Note that over-security consciousness can be risky if not done accurately and at the needed time. It can also stand as a weakness to your career and affect your job delivery. You must achieve it at an accurate level.

CHAPTER TWELVE

JOB AND HEALTH

Health can be a barrier to a worker's job and can be challenging if you do not take proper care of your health by following medical advice, getting regular checkups, and eating nutritious foods at the right times. Your body and health benefit from eating good food, which provides essential nutrients, keeps you fit for work, and improves your appearance, potentially encouraging your employer to offer you more opportunities. However, if you lack these nutrients for various reasons, your physical appearance can become a barrier to your job.

For workers to maintain good health, it begins with a healthy mind, which is crucial for nutrient absorption. When workers free themselves from excessive worry, even small amounts of food can provide significant nutrients. Conversely, constant stress can make problems seem insurmountable, leading to inner sickness, nutrient rejection, and an unattractive physical appearance, which can negatively impact job performance and opportunities.

Problems can act like a virus, harming your career through poor health if not properly addressed. This can render your job unprofitable and unprofessional, regardless of your experience or qualifications. Workers often face health challenges when their job demands more energy and power than their natural health, ability, and body weight can handle. In such cases, the job becomes too challenging or stressful, especially for those with health issues like body weight concerns, physical limitations, or lack of passion for the job. Many endure such jobs out of fear of unemployment or inability to compete, which can damage their emotional, physical, psychological, and mental health over time.

Some workers resort to alcohol, smoking, and hard drugs to cope with the physical demands of their jobs, hoping to boost their strength and increase their earnings. However, these substances gradually damage their health, leading to long-term pain and illness, which can be costly to treat and may result in serious health consequences or even death.

This reminds me of my university days when I was short on money for food and upkeep. The only way I could make money was by following a suggestion from my friend to join him in a construction job. He assured me that if I could set aside my shame, I would make money. I agreed.

On my first day at the construction site with my friend, I saw fellow students, which encouraged me. They explained the job and how the pay was based on the number of blocks carried, meaning the more you carry, the more you earn. As I started, I noticed some of my peers were already smoking and drinking alcohol upon arrival. I wondered how serious they were about the job, smoking and drinking before starting. I decided to stay focused.

My friend instructed me to start transferring blocks from where they were stacked to where they were needed; reminding me that my pay was based on how many I could carry. After transferring about thirty blocks, I became very weak and started sweating profusely, while my colleagues remained strong and fast. I wondered if I was the only one feeling tired, so I pretended and kept enduring. Eventually, I was too weak and started crying internally. My colleagues were still strong and steady.

I couldn't move my legs and had to rest before collapsing. I asked for sachet water, drinking and pouring it on my head. I asked the seller how many sachets I had taken, and she said fifteen, which wasn't surprising since I was still thirsty and very hungry. I quickly ordered and ate two plates of food while others continued working, strong and agile, with little water and no food.

I had to stop working because I had no strength left. That day, I ended up getting paid a small amount compared to my friend and other coworkers. I wondered why they didn't tire easily, knowing it was my first time. I believed they were human too, but I chose to focus on getting home because I was very weak. At home, I asked my friend why they didn't get tired. He smiled and said the job isn't easy and one needs to be strong. I asked what he meant, and he replied that drugs, smoking, and alcohol boost the body to make more money. He explained how these substances helped and paid off. I quickly recalled seeing them smoking, drinking, and taking drugs earlier, and I realized that was the reason.

The next morning, I couldn't stand up from bed due to strong pains all over my body. I realized that my body couldn't handle this kind of job, so I had to quit. If you find yourself unable to manage a job, have no passion for it, or lack motivation, you should definitely consider quitting. Some workers keep working in such jobs because they think they can't afford to lose a job or are afraid of being jobless, even when the job is harming them. This can gradually damage your emotions and health over time.

Workers need to understand that some jobs may not be suited for their body structure, body weight, or personality. To find a suitable job, consider and understand your health, body structure, body weight, and emotions before taking on any job.

Forcing yourself with determination, even when the job demands are beyond your physical capacity, is not advisable for health reasons. If you must continue, it requires gradual processing and learning to build your body to meet those demands. However, if your body isn't adapting quickly, it's advisable to stop the job; it simply isn't suitable for you.

CHAPTER THIRTEEN

WORKER'S PERSONAL PROBLEM

Problems are often found in human beings, mostly without learning or creating them; sometimes they come naturally. We notice some of us naturally have problematic manners and attitudes such as quick anger, hatred, lack of good approaches, inability to have a good attitude, etc., which rise to create problems in our jobs. Some of these problems develop naturally and become part of us.

The inability to discover these bad traits as workers can create problems in our day-to-day activities at work. These traits can gradually kill your job career and dreams despite your hard work. Noticing those characters that can cause headaches and bring problems is essential for finding solutions.

Workers are not born perfect, but the ability to learn and ask sincere questions will help you identify your flaws. Being open to learning and accepting corrections is a way to overcome traits that could hinder your career.

A friend of mine had a stubborn habit. After we graduated from secondary school, we found work at the same company. He kept acting stubbornly towards the supervisor's instructions. The supervisor always flagged it, and we often pleaded on his behalf. He never saw his stubborn habit as a problem. This caused constant issues between him and the supervisor, who kept reporting him to the manager. Despite his stubbornness, he was very effective and efficient in his work. He was one of the best in his department, but his attitude kept putting him in trouble. I did my best to help him, but there was only so much I could do.

Eventually, the company's sales and profits began dropping significantly. The management decided to reduce the number of workers to tackle the market and return to its sales shares. They explained their reasons, stating it was necessary due to ongoing bad sales. Workers who were not meeting their targets were let go, but my friend and I were lucky to stay. After a few months, the management assembled us again, indicating that more workers had to leave. Every remaining worker was a potential asset, making the decision difficult. They told each department to vote out three workers. I was voted in with some of my colleagues, but my friend was voted out.

When the management asked his department why they voted him out despite his excellent work, they said he was a troublemaker and a fighter. The management then allowed the department to decide his fate, resulting in his dismissal. His inability to recognize his stubbornness as a problem led to his termination, despite being one of the best workers. His stubborn attitude turned him into a troublemaker and fighter, causing him to lose respect and love from his colleagues.

As workers, always see yourself as imperfect, even when you or your company thinks you are great. Be open to learning, corrections, and adjustments in all you do. Understand yourself and never let others see your willingness to learn as a weakness.

INTRA-PERSONAL PROBLEM

These intra-personal problems are issues found within oneself as a worker, created and developed through attitudes such as lack of proper approach, poor manners, and quickness to anger, impatience, and violence. These traits are detrimental and can be seen as self-imposed barriers to one's dreams and job career. This backwardness is a problem within oneself, especially when there is a lack of self-control and management.

Finding yourself in these kinds of problems can make you unhappy and a failure at work, regardless of your best abilities. I seldom advise workers to understand their intra-personal problems and learn how to manage and control them if they want to be great in their job and career.

INTER PERSONAL PROBLEM

These are problems created among workers and transferred from one worker to another; these types of problems usually occur at the workplace, and their nature can be triggered by your boss's decisions, unpaid salary, or unacceptable ways of doing the job and workers' differences. You usually leave home happily, only to arrive at work and notice some negative impression that brings problems, probably from your boss, your co-worker, or the job itself. This tends to affect your happiness and create differences among you, your workers, your boss, and the company as a whole.

These types of problems make workers unhappy for the day and kill passion for the job at the moment. Failure to control yourself and try to promote unity at the very moment might cost you productivity and damage your job reputation because it will make you lose focus.

JOB AS A PROBLEM

The job itself can also be the reason for having problems with oneself. When the job seems very challenging or burdensome, especially when you lose passion for it for reasons best known to you, it becomes unbearable and very difficult to deliver with an unhappy mind. In this case, it is usually advisable to set your mind on good and workable things to revive your passion. If you find the job more harmful and your lack of passion seems very strong to the extent that it might or has started affecting your psychology, physical health, or even your freedom, it will be very good for you to stop the job and go for one where you will find passion and freedom. If not, it will give way to producing negative attitudes that will hurt you emotionally, health-wise, and bring more negative tags from colleagues.

I keep advocating for friends, co-workers, and colleagues that wherever they are experiencing more pain than pleasure, lack passion and confidence despite how hard they try to be better, and probably not seeing a future in that job, they should quickly quit such a job. All you keep gaining are results of emotional pain, high risk of health deterioration, and in most cases, you keep remitting your salary back to the job by paying for damages incurred, salary reductions as prompted, and lack of self-belief.

In some cases, you can notice having passion for one job, but your health or body structure is not accommodating such a job by making you fall ill often or causing health deficiencies. It is also in your best interest to get another job that balances your health emotionally, physically, and mentally.

FAMILY PROBLEM

These kinds of problems often affect workers' ability to perform their jobs effectively. These issues typically occur in family settings due to differences that lead to worker unhappiness, making it difficult to deliver quality work. Such problems preoccupy the worker's mind, creating psychological burdens that impact their professional performance. There is a saying that a happy family is a healthier family. Failure to maintain a happy family life can diminish job effectiveness. These problems vary and are found within the worker's family, contributing to a lack of ability to deliver work uniquely.

The truth about life is that some family problems should not be dwelled upon at the workplace, as they can weaken one's ability to deliver. It requires knowledge to manage these problems without letting them dominate one's thoughts at work. When these issues become overwhelming, it is essential to find solutions quickly before they jeopardize your job. One of the best ways to handle these problems is to focus on solutions rather than dwelling on the problems themselves. Even while seeking solutions, don't let the problem take full charge of your working thoughts. You can temporarily manage at work by engaging in fun, current affairs, politics, and sports discussions with co-workers, which can help you deliver for the day.

Your working wisdom is the ability to use your thoughts effectively through thinking, researching, learning, creating, and innovating. Even a minor disturbance in thought can prevent you from performing at your best. Workers are encouraged to stay focused and use their wisdom to excel in their jobs because failure to do so may result in their credits going to co-workers and discouragement in their field.

I heard a story about a couple who got married a few years ago. Misunderstandings and quarrels began to manifest, leading to unresolved issues because they focused on the problems rather than solving them. This became unbearable for the husband, who could not concentrate or focus on his job. The problem constantly occupied his thoughts, preventing him from meeting job challenges. A friend advised him not to let the problem ruin his job, but the man said he didn't care about anything except dealing with his wife. For six months, his company's board and management evaluated his performance, finding his contributions lacking. Consequently, they had to take immediate action by sacking him, despite his role as head of the sales and marketing department. He couldn't believe his eyes, as he never thought of losing his job. The problem that led to his dismissal remained, generating more issues. Eventually, he ended up divorced and jobless, having lost his position as a top officer in sales and marketing.

CHAPTER FOURTEEN

TRIBALISM AND NEPOTISM

Jobs in Nigeria are few in industries as a result of self-interest and the system in which Nigerians run their political and government affairs. Predictions have it that Nigerian workers will pay more in the hands of their employers due to the gradual reduction of industries with political power and multiple taxes, which have inflated unemployment and left many small and medium enterprises and industries with no option but to close down businesses. Only political businesses and industries can survive this, causing significant issues in the labor economy despite the claim of one nation, one country in unity. There are differences that affect the unity of labor citizenship. Being a laborer in Nigeria, a worker must understand these national differences to cope and work effectively. These differences can be advantageous or disadvantageous to enable workers to carry out their job.

Tribe and tribalism have been significant challenges workers face in carrying out their duties. Tribalism also determines who gets the job irrespective of qualifications. In this system, employment is often determined by the employer's tribe, family, and power. Employees must connect with the employer's tribe, family, or power. Consequently, vital posts and offices are filled by those connected in some way. If connected to power, it means the employee might be a hardcore loyalist or a candidate backed by someone with absolute power over the employer, leaving the employer no choice but to fill the position without objection.

In other cases where employment has been outsourced to human resources (HR) companies to fill vacant offices, after all is said and done, the majority tribe in the company might group and partner against minority tribes. They partner with the HR Company to determine who is to be employed by slotting their tribe's candidate to the HR Company. HR companies may not effectively control and limit these challenges, compromising to maintain partnerships and please powerful bosses.

Nepotism and patronage have made it difficult for qualified workers to secure good jobs. Employers often favor relatives or personal friends over more capable candidates. The limited space of available jobs forces workers to connect with influential patrons to gain access to good jobs, knowing nepotism can get them very far in the world. This reliance on connections rather than abilities and knowledge is growing, leading to increased loyalty to powerful patrons.

The problems of tribalism and nepotism affect company growth by preventing the hiring of capable workers who could contribute to the company's growth. This affects workers' prospects of getting good jobs, compromises their abilities during interviews, and impacts the economy by encouraging laziness and creating ghost workers. High levels of fraud can result from selling vacant offices to the highest bidder, reducing the discovery of new talents and increasing the focus on connections.

The annoying part of this system is the questions employers ask during interviews to secure positions for their own purposes, such as "You are here in respect of whom?" "Who brought you here?" "Who informed you about the job?" They know the job wasn't advertised, and they ask, "What tribe are you?" "Can you speak the language?" This reflects a biased hiring process driven more by connections than by genuine skill and talent.

www.ingramcontent.com/pod-product-compliance
Lightning Source LLC
Chambersburg PA
CBHW020440220526
45464CB00002B/792